T0167245

An
Approach
to Style That
Promises
Power, Money, and Class

An
Approach
to Style That
Promises
Power, Money, and Class

PALLE AND LYNDIA SMIDT

AN APPROACH TO STYLE THAT PROMISES POWER, MONEY, AND CLASS

iUniverse books may be ordered through booksellers or by contacting:

iUniverse
1663 Liberty Drive
Bloomington, IN 47403
www.iuniverse.com
1-800-Authors (1-800-288-4677)

ISBN: 978-1-4917-9839-3 (sc)
ISBN: 978-1-4917-9840-9 (e)

Library of Congress Control Number: 2016912382

Print information available on the last page.

iUniverse rev. date: 01/31/2017

Contents

Introduction.. vii

Part 1. The Management Environment 1

1. Stakes and Career.. 3
2. Salesmanship...10
3. Leadership and the Managerial Imperative.............. 13
4. Strategy versus Tactics.. 23

Part 2. Safeguards against Deceptive Thinking.............31

5. Clear Thinking 33
6. Propaganda and Suggestion......................................35
7. Dishonest Tricks in Argument................................. 41

Part 3. Ethics 49

8. Integrity...51
9. Promise Keeping 55
10. Loyalty.. 57
11. What Not to Do... 59

Part 4. Good Manners 63

12. Tactfulness and Good Manners 65
13. Day-to-Day Rules of Etiquette 67

14. Rules of Etiquette for Parties and Entertaining....... 83
15. Visiting Cards and Telephoning.............................112
16. Traveling Abroad.. 115

Conclusion 127

References 129

Index.. 133

Introduction

People worry about how to survive and excel in the workplace. Personal choices come under scrutiny. Many tend to elaborate on their personal histories or past successes, emphasizing instances where their knowledge or actions have been key in outdistancing their rivals. Clearly, such elaboration has often proved itself a formula for success. However, more than this is necessary to ensure ongoing success. What is needed comes in the form of knowing what to do when interacting and working with others. This knowing is what we call *style.*

We have all experienced that insight and effort alone do not automatically result in arriving at the most satisfactory solution. There can be many reasons for this; one is that we were unable to influence others; consequently, smart people are often left out. To avoid that, we decided to write this book to examine some obvious opportunities readily available to all of us—opportunities that are peripheral to the practice of doing work but at the same time crucial to success. With that in mind, we found it important to discuss a few key characteristics of the business environment, such as *career, winning, leadership, committees, management behavior, strategy,* and *tactics.* We chose these topics because choices as to deployment of assets and people are frequently less than optimum, or just plain wrong, which points to the need for a convincing style to sort out what makes sense. In other words, style provides the key to effectiveness, and true effectiveness leads to lasting success.

When dealing with colleagues, both friends and foes, on matters for solution, we know all too well that they often inject irrelevant emotion and self-serving politics into their arguments. We shall address such attempts to sidetrack rational methods of thought, offering solutions to avoid ending up at the losing end and becoming party to adopting conclusions that risk our rendering ourselves useless.

Further, we shall round off what we hope to be helpful hints by addressing ethics and trustworthiness, which we consider of paramount importance to success, professionally as well as socially.

Finally, another element essential to style—or class—is to treat all people with respect, simply by being courteous and polite. In covering that subject, this book easily turns into a rule book. Use it as such, but remember that the rules do not always have to be followed literally. That said, however, the rules must be mastered in order to gain others' respect and support, without which real success may elude us.

The objective of this book is thus twofold: (1) to create a style that complements effectively the material form and technical know-how of our professional pursuits, and (2) to give advice conducive to creating an enviable, distinguishable personality that is difficult for rivals to duplicate in short order.

PART 1

The Management Environment

1

Stakes and Career

The Stakes

In a world where business as usual is no longer a viable option, the assessment of the stakes should be based on the understanding that the real stakes involve the ultimate realization of an individual's capacity to succeed. The right choices should not be made on the basis of conventional wisdom. Rather, it is essential to identify what must be done to make feasible that which is personally necessary, as this is what can truly make a difference. We suggest that the most important area to focus on is personal conduct, or style. Why? The answer is simple. Without paying attention to style, we will be unable to effectively confront the deep-seated challenges to our individual competitive positions. The solution is to know and apply the rules of conduct and also to know what pitfalls we may face and how to handle them. True, there are many other critical issues involved in business and career planning, and we do not advocate sidestepping them. However, combining business know-how with increased awareness of conduct will make each of us a formidable competitor in the job market and a sought-after member in the social arena. It will reduce or eliminate barriers to carrying through plans and proposals. It will reduce or eliminate unproductive confrontations, and ultimately, it will favorably impact personal success rates. Indeed, developing an attractive, distinguishable style is risk-free; even more important, it eliminates risk.

Career

To base the advancement of your career exclusively on performance, in regard to direct industrial or political matters, is a very difficult strategy. It is a tough road to take, and it only works if performance is there at all times—and even then, there is no guarantee of success. Why? Because politics is as prevalent in business as it is in government. Favoritism is the order of the day, and competitive threats in terms of employee performance are not always welcome. The territorial imperative is in full force. And the good-ol'-boy system flourishes. It is difficult to become part of the inner circle, which in many businesses and government is almost exclusively male. On the surface the guys may be friendly, but that does not exclude the possibility that they will stab you in the back. The way to survive in such an environment is to be pleasant and smarter than the others.

You rise to power most easily by sticking to the familiar pattern: high grades for admission to a prominent university, leading to a sought-after degree, both which in turn lead to the right career with the right business or institution. This is still the ordinary recipe for bringing about affluence.

Unfortunately, the likelihood of achieving maximum performance from any cliquish system or from self-preservation is quite remote, since the most important feature is "to belong." Businesses and governments have often been known to strive for leaders like the so-called company man, a clone of others who seek to belong, because such environments favor conformity. In such circumstances, it is possible that the profit or performance motive will be pushed into the background. That means the organization is less tolerant of mavericks, and the most competent individuals are not allowed to rise quickly.

The question still remains as to whether there are certain routes to top positions which are smoother and less time consuming than others. For instance, is it better to take the engineering route as compared to sales or finance? The answer has very much to do with the mind-set of the hiring company.

For the sake of simplification, let's group companies into three categories. The first is the *hunter,* the organization constantly looking for business in which volume is key. The second is the *farmer,* a structure which always wants endless quantitative measures in place before feeling comfortable to proceed, and in which analysis often becomes more important than the action to be taken from it. The third is the *shepherd,* an organization which is custodial in nature. Thus, a business which has sales as its top priority resembles the hunter. A business primarily run by engineers has the characteristics of the farmer (everything gets measured minutely). Finally, a company which constantly seeks comfort in the status quo, such as serving relentlessly the installed product and customer base instead of also pursuing new business vigorously, has the traits of the shepherd. At the risk of oversimplifying, it is tougher for an employee with the traits of a hunter to succeed swiftly in a company characterized as a farmer. Such categories cannot be ignored: they constitute the corporate culture of the organization in question.

That said, here is an observation on general management: To work toward the top is a clear goal for many in business as well as in politics. To decide on relevant business positioning in terms of where and when to place assets, and at what levels, is a most critical management function.

The foregoing observation leads to an important exercise for general management: how to despecialize the specialist. Remember that the route to the top is by way of specialization. But the specialist's actions may not be conducive to creating wealth for the owners of the business. Despecialization does not work if it results in diluting functional know-how. In fact, the exact opposite is required: namely, that the general manager is at home in all major aspects of the business, preferably with such familiarity obtained through a career path involving responsibility for a multitude of various operating entities and functions over a period of time.

In short, the despecialization of the specialist becomes productive when it takes place by means of elevating his or her know-how in related areas; after which an overall balanced approach can be executed in general management, with full understanding as to what creates wealth. Knowing that the trade-offs are tough should be nothing but motivating.

It is easy to see why interpersonal skills, such as individual style of communication and conduct, may become the overarching element that transforms potential performers into superstars. Style, at best, results in something unique but hard to measure, although it is very recognizable. This is where we leave solid ground. Not that rules of conduct are mysterious; on the contrary. But when somebody is considered to have an attractive style—whether in conduct or communication—is there any assurance that it is relevant to performance and that it can be learned and duplicated over and over again? To a large degree, the answer is yes.

Winning

So how do we win in this personal race? Winning is an individual as well as a collective issue. Let's briefly examine what the issue is for a company so that we can put our personal performance in the right context. In the aggregate, *winning* is essential from a business, economic, and national-security point of view, so that our country may achieve dominant positions in industries vital to future prospects. This scenario has political undertones, but let's concentrate here on what makes up the aggregate: the individual company.

For most managers, to win means to be number one in product-markets. Normally, that means to prevail over rivals in the competition for market share, with the concurrent goal of being the low-cost producer. To win in the product-markets also implies such things as holding a technology lead, maintaining superior quality, and so forth. This focus on winning is understandable, but it points toward a more fundamental question: What criterion should we use to measure success in business? Or, to put this another way, what does it mean to win in business?

The underlying premise is that companies participate in two markets: the product-market and the capital-market. Excessive emphasis on the narrow product-market view of winning, and the consequent lack of emphasis on the capital-market view of winning, has been a major factor in the failure of many businesses to generate new wealth for their shareholders.

Indeed, when combined with an uncritical preoccupation with growth, the narrow product-market view of winning has resulted in businesses implementing strategies which often confiscate wealth at a startling rate. Why has this happened? There are three major reasons. First, too little attention has been paid to what the customer needs and wants, in particular where such requirements differ from region to region in the global market. Second, many managers have no model of the linkage between strategy and warranted value. Management often does not understand that there is no general rule which links product-market victories to value creation for a company's shareholders. Increasing market share, rapid growth, and investment to achieve a low-cost position may add value, but clearly, it could also confiscate value. Shareholders are not romantics; they don't care if product-market strategies all result in being number one in any narrow sense of relative share or cost position. On the contrary, investors are very pragmatic; if they do not see capital gains resulting from a particular business strategy, they will not raise their estimate of the value of a company's common stock, which is the true yardstick of winning. Third, failure to adopt the capital-market view of winning and to develop product-market strategies accordingly, which in turn assures that value-reducing, rather than value-maximizing, strategies will continue to be selected and implemented.

So here we are. When the company we work for wins, we win also. But do we? Sure we do, if we simultaneously advance in the company's ranks, achieve more responsibility, more power, more recognition overall, and more pay. This adds an important dimension to personal winning; it should preferably be realized in a winning environment, not a losing one.

In the next chapter, we will discuss the skill of salesmanship, a dynamic that impacts all effective management and all successful careers in business.

2

Salesmanship

There is hardly a group that is more examined and more analyzed than managers. The focus is always on how to perform. That traditionally centers on how to move products and how to move people, and includes the framework necessary to perform the tasks. Workers—subordinates, peers, and bosses—must be motivated. Therefore, everybody needs salesmanship, especially in an environment where there are conflicts and competition galore.

The fundamentals of salesmanship can be learned. The quality and effectiveness of its application are key. To be proficient, it is necessary to master all facets leading to the closing of an order, whether a customer order or a resolution at a management meeting.

The bottom line must be dealt with at the onset. That means starting with the best answer and the best approach. Early on, it is essential to create interest; do not hesitate to use the trial close whenever it makes sense. Other facets to be dealt with are reasoning, examples, judging probabilities, and assessing rejected options, showing all sides of each issue fairly and thereby increasing the chances of arriving at a sound and acceptable conclusion. Answering objections is an important part of moving toward the summary and the close. Always make sure to be crisp and brief, and if arguments or material need not be covered, eliminate them.

Salesmanship also relies on suggestion. The psychological facet of suggestion is that if statements are made again and again in a confident manner, without arguments and proof, listeners will tend to believe them quite independently of their soundness and the presence or absence of evidence of their truth. Most especially, listeners will tend to accept the suggestions of the speaker if he or she has the acknowledged dignity of authority. It is regrettable that many persons unjustly attempt to be perceived as having prestige, using any means necessary to achieve that perception. The salesperson, the administrator, the politician, and the propagandist all are usually ready to exploit all tendencies that make people more suggestible. Specialists with one form of expertise are obvious targets of specialists with another form of expertise.

To master the process is not enough. It must be applied often to achieve productivity. Articulation of clear positions is not enough. Those positions must be worked through and translated into real terms, in ways that would help convince others. Many reaffirm their positions without paying attention to making it happen bureaucratically. In any case, salesmanship is not a monologue. We should never lose sight of the ability to ask the right questions that will serve the person well, in terms of eliciting the relevant information he or she requires. It is worthwhile to remember that when confronted with the request to authorize action, tenure, common sense, compartmental knowledge, and orchestrated, undeserved authority are by no means exempt from questioning. Nevertheless, in business as well as in politics, judgment is regularly passed on these bases.

Let's keep in mind what is really important when it comes to salesmanship. The order of the day is that selling has a running contest with adversity. Anyone can react swiftly to rivals' quantitative changes and deceptive tricks, but what cannot be combated without delay is superior salesmanship. It gets ideas across. It finalizes matters, and it clearly defines style.

With the skills of salesmanship mastered, we are ready to apply our style as successful leader, and leadership is the topic covered in the next chapter.

3

Leadership and the Managerial Imperative

Leadership

Leadership is motivating followers to execute the goals set for them. This definition is key to the proper understanding of leadership. Leadership is about operating acumen. It is about understanding businesses, products and services, competition, and risk. It requires putting together the right team and having the common sense to listen to and involve others.

Not all goals can be hand-me-down targets. Employees and workers must be consulted. Decision making often requires considerable consensus building. Sometimes it is not useful to seek consensus, as such seeking can be very time consuming. Many proposals and ideas are clearly better than others, which can shorten the decision-making process. But that does not justify managers being tyrants and alienating their subordinates. We need to take into account the way in which subordinates are inspired and motivated, as well as the way in which they accept and act on directions from leaders. Sound leadership further requires that subordinates' performance be assessed against stipulated goals that are clear and that support competitive advantage, shareholder value, and corporate values. Understanding of the goals does not constitute leadership; subordinates must be encouraged, and the goals must be realized.

It is significant to accept that leadership is very much a binary issue. Either the goals are met (or exceeded), or they are not. Good leaders meet the expectations or the goal; bad ones do not. This leads to an important aspect of leadership; namely goal setting itself. By our definition, outstanding leadership can be deployed in relation to bad objectives or poor fundamentals. That the goals and the followers may be bad does not necessarily make the leader bad as well; a case in point could be a turnaround situation. Consequently, we shall deduce that good leadership can be executed on bad goals, but not for long. Both corporate and political history show numerous examples of this. Another downside risk inherent in leadership is that the means to achieve an end may not be good. That happens repeatedly. Therefore, to achieve meaningful leadership in business, as well as in politics, goal setting becomes critical; tough goals make a good manager creative. In business, that means the goals at the corporate level must maximize wealth creation, and at lower levels they must contribute to such wealth creation.

One of the most common flaws in leadership is failing to assume responsibility. For instance, hardly anything undermines the overall position of a manager more than unpleasant or tough conclusions communicated to subordinates as being upper-management or head-office decisions. The manager who does this usually phrases it as, "It is not my decision." Regardless of how or by whom a manager receives authorization to act, such action must be communicated to subordinates as management's position or decision, not somebody else's. Every manager must demonstrate alignment with upper management. Another typical example is a manager who excuses the company to the subordinate by explaining to the worker that the corporate office did not agree with the recommended salary increase. This puts upper management in a bad light when the actual salary increase is less than the manager's recommendation. It also makes the manager subject to being ignored by subordinates. Remember President Truman: "The buck stops here." Again, alignment with upper management is always key. A good manager may disagree with upper management on important matters—say, next year's proposed operating plan—but when the planning session is finished and a plan has been agreed to, that manager must implement it as if it were his own plan, not as a compromise that the corporate office forced him to accept. To put this another way, a manager may often disagree with upper management on pending issues, but the moment those issues are decided upon, that manager must implement the agreed-upon plan as if it were his or her own plan—without quarrel and without any underhandedness. When changes prove necessary, of course they must be made; however, a unified management front is essential. That is how real teamwork functions in management.

If upper management repeatedly makes wrong decisions, a manager has no option other than to seek employment elsewhere. No manager can afford to be associated with defeat. The other side of the coin is *hierarchical exfoliation* (as defined by Peter and Hull in *The Peter Principle*), where supercompetence is more objectionable than incompetence because supercompetence destroys the hierarchy. A super competent manager should, as a rule, become associated with a super competent company or institution, unless such a manager can become associated as a top executive with an incompetent or moderately competent company, in which case he or she would be able to call the shots.

People who display leadership apply it to meaningful, important tasks, and they understand what is required for success. In other words, they find realistic ways to get the job done, and they work hard at it. In doing so, they establish organizations and structures in which people can succeed. A quantification of management by level of competence is likely to show a heavily skewed bell-shaped curve, meaning that large numbers are less than moderately competent. Such skewing is relevant to style. Many industrial psychologists and managers love to give opinions on how to become an effective leader. The suggested solutions mostly deal in routine issues, sidestepping the essential reality that the key elements of good leadership are often created during the formative years, and are, consequently, difficult to duplicate.

Management by Committee

Another aspect of the management environment and the decision-making process that we must consider is *management by committee.* Both the public and private sectors love committees. This is despite the fact that many productive people consider the committee approach to be a waste of time, particularly because movers and shakers do not like processes that are incremental, time consuming, and achieved by consensus.

So why do we have more committees than necessary? Why do we have larger committees than necessary? The answer is simple: lack of leadership and lack of confident management. More so than anything else, insecurity combined with congenial fluffiness are the predominant reasons for advocating excessive committees and committee membership.

Since committees occupy an arena in which style becomes important, let's take a brief moment to discuss how to modify the framework of the committee process so that it contributes to effectiveness and eliminates some of the pitfalls thereto. First and foremost, we must distinguish between meetings that are necessary for decision making and those whose objective is information sharing.

Committees form a battleground where it is tough to win without paying close attention to the issues we caution you about throughout this book. It is easy to be sidetracked or outmaneuvered in the committee forum. Consequently, it is helpful when important subjects for committee consideration are approached in a somewhat formalistic manner, which of course does not shut the door on situations where managers like to hear their colleagues debate options for decision making in small, rather informal get-togethers. There, the open process and live discussion as follow-up to brief memos may fairly highlight the relevance of opposing views. The more formalistic manner does streamline things, and it also defuses emotional and less-rational opponents. The emphasis should be on providing timely and adequate background material and obtaining proper staff reviews for matters going to committee. For items where advance preparation is needed, the agenda must be distributed in advance of the scheduled meeting. It should list the topics to be covered, the time allowed for each presentation, the presenters, and the other attendees. Alternatively, the agenda can be built live from the current foreground concerns of the committee members (if so, these should be separated into decision items and information items). For action items, written background material must be provided in advance of the meeting, and such material should be of sufficient depth to provide the committee with an accurate understanding of the key issues involved and the rationale for the proposed course of action. The background material should be accompanied by a review summary sheet stating what action the committee is asked to take. Except in unusual circumstances, reviews should be canceled if adequate background material is not provided on time. It is worth noting that most boards of directors do not want to make decisions; they want to approve or reject proposals. This distinction may seem subtle, but it is important.

The department sponsoring the presentation requesting action or approval is responsible for obtaining the reviews and comments of other departments, as appropriate, prior to the meeting so that all information needed for an informed appraisal of the subject matter is available. The intent should be to focus the formal review on key aspects of the subject matter, with the details covered in the written background material, as noted above. Appropriate documentation for conclusions, agreements or actions to be taken as a result of the meeting must be maintained in the form of committee meeting minutes, and in some cases, a supplementary letter to the sponsoring department. The committee secretary will be responsible for dealing with departments on follow-up requests and for scheduling response reviews, which may be recommended by the committee.

Committees are normally not for educational purposes, but rather, for running the business; therefore, limit the attendance. Modern technology, such as the Internet and satellite-based communications networks, has largely changed this landscape.

From a pragmatic point of view, committees, whether decision-making or advisory, tax the style of their members. Uncouth, confrontational behavior is bound to fall short, and pushiness supported by trade competence alone will hardly sway the listeners. Tact, in addition to business know-how, therefore becomes a sought-after commodity. The committee setting is where challenges are plentiful, and where mistakes are striking.

The Managerial Imperative

In examining employee behaviors in hierarchical systems it is useful to revisit *Parkinson's Law* and *The Peter Principle.* Parkinson formulated his law before Peter developed his principle; therefore, it is not surprising that Peter rejects many aspects of Parkinson's Law of *staff accumulation in hierarchies.* Peter opposes the theory that senior employees practice a strategy of divide and conquer when it comes to staff aggregation. His argument is that many senior employees are incapable of formulating any effective plans for division, conquest, or any other purpose. He further argues that overstaffing and underproduction, as described by Parkinson, are often directly opposed to the interests of supervisory and managerial personnel. (Although he had a coauthor [Hull] for the book *The Peter Principle,* Peter developed his principle prior to the book's publication, so we refer to him singly throughout when referring to the Peter Principle.)

Peter goes on to explain why there is no direct relationship between the size of the staff and the amount of useful work. According to the Peter Principle, every employee in a hierarchy tends to rise to his or her level of incompetence. Peter also argues against *Parkinson's pyramid,* which puts limitations on hierarchical forms. (Parkinson made his discovery in the armed forces, where obsolete traditions and modes of organization have the strongest foothold.)

As students of the workings of institutions, both Parkinson and Peter advanced very valuable ideas. Who is right—or primarily right—is really not that important. It is essential to understand that Peter, in particular, seems too optimistic in regard to the ways in which employees deliberately pursue efficiency. But even more important, the *level of incompetence* is a default condition which makes the Peter Principle fail on the following grounds. First, it is based on a view that everything may be proceeding reasonably well, until the level of incompetence is reached. Experience in the real world presents a different picture. Competence versus incompetence is a capability issue, and as such, it is certainly important. But the impediment to doing useful work is rather pedestrian; moreover, it is based not on a default condition but on intent and design. Second, in pursuit of more power and more responsibility, some employees may be risk takers, a phenomenon which often falters when the same employees' territorial responsibility increases.

Nevertheless, lack of risk taking is a willful act. People normally do not want to venture into the unfamiliar— not because they (eventually) cannot get their arms around the opportunity or the problem, but because errors of omission are less transparent and less ascribable than errors of commission.

Therefore, we need to bring forward another law, or principle, which we call *the Managerial Imperative,* or *the Palle Principle*: in a hierarchy, every manager tends to rise to his or her level of indecision.

This is a real reason for lack of performance, where something necessary is delayed or simply ignored. Competence is often present, or it can be acquired, but lack of commitment cripples progress. The employee focuses on how much he or she may gain or lose through an involvement or a concession, instead of concentrating on what the company may gain or lose by moving forward. This notion is key to understanding hierarchical behavior and performance. It takes every skill in the style toolkit for a supercompetent achiever to deal convincingly and effectively with individuals who adhere to the Managerial Imperative.

Now that we have a clearer understanding of leadership and management, let's move on to strategy and tactics, which we will explore in the next chapter.

4

Strategy versus Tactics

A never-ending discussion in business has centered on whether strategy or tactics impact results most favorably, or whether it is more important to make the right choices in terms of content as opposed to method. In other words, which is more important: strategy (the "what") or tactics (the "how")?

In government, the issue is the same. Here, the distinction is between policy, on the one hand, which reflects chosen strategies, and laws, regulations, and resource deployment, on the other hand, all of which equate to tactics. In business, top executives do strategic planning, which parallels the considerable time that branches of government devote to policy matters.

In practice, the borderline between strategy and tactics is often blurred. Choice of positioning is strategic, whereas execution is tactical. There is no doubt that it is far easier to bring forward ideas and proposals as to what strategy to adopt than to implement the plans successfully. Many a good thinker can do the former, especially in the abstract, but it takes great management to produce exceptional results.

It is doubly hard to execute effective tactics because of the flat learning curve that tactics engender, which stem from management's task to "move" both people and merchandise.

Since promoting ideas does not require a solid track record in operations, it comes as no surprise that many managers, particularly staff management, desire to contribute to every debate on strategy formulation.

To develop important strategic plans that can be translated into effective tactics, which in turn can deliver the necessary results, encompasses the very essence of enterprise. When, through the right strategic choices, good economic fundamentals are present in a business, even average or mediocre operations management will look good.

But if a company does not enjoy substantial advantages because of its business strategy, it had better know how to effectively run its day-to-day operations. In short; this is where tactics become king. Poorly thought-out strategies and mediocre tactics will never suffice in such situations. However, the real question is, what would do the least damage: poor strategy or poor tactics?

The answer is poor strategy, because brilliant execution can offset most planning deficiencies, but even the best of strategies will not produce the required results if execution is pathetic. For the up-and-coming manager, the dialogue on setting a course and choosing the means of implementation can become so heated that a flawless style and conduct is essential to persevering.

A lot of errors in judgment have impacted strategy formulation. What were some of the things that went wrong?

They were many, but let's enumerate the best examples. Business units were often defined as *product programs.* The introduction of what was called the *experience curve* was a fad. *Capital allocation,* as described by the growth- and market-share matrix, was a fundamental economic misconception, where solution attempts required invidious comparisons, simultaneity, and credulity. The *balanced cash flows* concept is still well and alive. *Strategic planning* has often drowned in implementation details; it often became "financial planning" in elaborate organizations whose only real product was paperwork that attempted to reduce uncertainties by pure analytical effort. (Manuals are no substitute for thinking and priority setting. Start with a blank piece of paper; it is not impossible to settle on a sound strategy.)

An example from government that reveals flaws in strategic thinking and debatable tactical choices is *industrial policy,* the premise of which is based on the belief that markets and the private sector are incapable of dealing with our economic industrial problems and that government should step in. When the Berlin Wall came down, it exposed the collapse of centrally planned economies. But the concept is by no means dead, as evidenced when applied to subsets of the economy with too many regulations. Large number of industries in the past were laid open to similar arguments, as is also evidenced in today's dialogue on downsizing, offshoring (moving jobs abroad), protectionism, and so on. Bringing back foreign manufacturing jobs, helped by government intrusion in the ordinary functioning of the private marketplace, is doomed to fail. Capital intensity in industry and cost of capital will be key to winning, not the restoring of the factory worker of past. Government must bring about a framework that gets rid of roadblocks for business, both domestically and in the global marketplace. One such impediment is the tax code that needs a complete overhaul, and another is the wrong approach to money. Let's not forget the so-called other side of the coin: what if foreign governments drew interventionist conclusions similar to those suggested above? The consequences would be unthinkable, and they would lead to economic chaos, as foreign investments and associated jobs in the United States would be cut back or eliminated.

Advocates of industrial policy, in an attempt to be afforded special privileges, let their desires lead them to accept a belief by constructing an apparently rational set of reasons for supposing that belief to be true. The reasons are mere rationalizations of notions held on irrational grounds. At the very least, we must constantly pay attention to arguments ignoring that what is true of one or more parts of a whole, taken separately, is not necessarily true of the whole; and conversely, that what is true of the whole is not necessarily true of the parts taken separately. The fallacy arising from neglect of such rules is well illustrated in this passage (source: Jepson, R. W. 1954., *Clear Thinking*. London: Longman's, Green and Co.).

> Modern technology is able to create continually
> greater wealth with the employment of fewer
> persons and, so far as the majority of them

> are concerned, less skilled persons. This means that a smaller proportion of the total wealth is distributed in wages and salaries, and that, as the bulk of our population maintains itself out of wage and salary earnings, the majority of the people receive a proportionally smaller share of the total social product.

The first sentence applies to certain industries, in particular, and not to industry as a whole; in general, the aggregate employment tends to increase under stable economic circumstances. The second sentence applies to *total wealth,* the argument which has been made for the benefit of particular industries only, and which ignores (1) the often vast increase in the total wealth of a country, and (2) the increasing number of new industries. Other fallacies include people forgetting that circumstances alter cases, tampering with the premises upon which the conclusions about to be deduced have been based, making circular arguments, ignoring the point at hand, and engaging in extension and diversion.

It is easy to see how fact can be turned into fable by not only manipulating the matter itself but also using questionable forms of argument. (We shall deal with that in part 2.) Unassailable logic will not always suffice. Most people accept this, but only as theory. Either way, a do-nothing approach can be persuasive, as we saw in the Managerial Imperative (see chapter 3). The waste in business and government is staggering. Plenty of analysis but, all too often, no meaningful plan. We have modeled the world to death on many irrelevant issues.

What is the point of all this? It is twofold: (1) planning fascinates many employees over and over again, and (2) some people have gone from the do-nothing theory to doing too much too fast, without necessarily solving the most important problems. Each idea is like Pandora's box once opened: empty.

Clearly, top management favors the contention process to sort out the important must-do projections. To that end, another aspect is added: namely, staff reviews. They are designated in order to achieve the dual objectives of ensuring that all pertinent perspectives are applied to matters that must be transacted, as well as assisting the individual approver to have maximum comprehension of all facets of the transaction he or she is approving. Any transaction that establishes policy or precedent, or that impacts on other organization activities, is subject to staff reviews, besides what is inherent in policy and procedural guides to delineate delegation of authority for management. The basic premise of any approval schedule is that delegated authority—which extends vertically, not horizontally—bears with it the obligation to exercise sound discretion and good business judgment. Thus, strategy versus tactics and line versus staff will surface every need for productive conduct along the lines described herein. Also, safeguard attending the important meetings ("out of the room, out of the deal," so to speak). Start concentrating on the here and now, at least as a stepping-stone. The present is more available than either memories of the past or fantasies of the future; know what is happening, and remain unbiased, clear, and down-to-earth.

Few people realize how repetitive, and hence automatic, the vast majority of everyday thinking is. Consider that direct observation on the part of colleagues is often faulty; their sources of information may be unreliable or not relevant, and their inferences may be inaccurate. Therefore, do the homework, do not spring surprises on anybody, and go through the checks-and-balances process prior to sending proposals up the organization. When less-than-straightforward thinking is combined with a specialist's work expertise, arguments can become very combative. In such circumstances, tact very quickly becomes a virtue.

Striving to clear the scene of strategy versus tactics brings to mind what Winston Churchill once said: "It is always more easy to discover and proclaim general principles than to apply them." It is clear, however, that without its best strategy, a business will not optimize its performance.

Where does that leave us? Much energy is expended on budgeting operations, often with meaningless or irrelevant guidance from strategic planning, where strategy formulation may be messy, resulting in a general statement of intent, a set of financial objectives, a multiple scenario analysis, a forecast of the future with plenty of room for the intuitive and the subjective, or any combination thereof. As previously indicated, this is a bad definition of strategy.

On the contrary, we must ensure that business value depends upon expected future cash flows, properly discounted. An actionable plan (maximum thirty to thirty-five pages and minimum amount of financial data) for the business (unit or total) dealing with a few specific competitors is necessary, and from plausible alternatives the one of highest value should be selected; further, the capital required to implement that strategy should be committed to and funded in a way that involves organization, resource allocation (capital and other), and business development.

Now it is no longer strategy versus tactics. It is competent versus incompetent general managers! Being smart and informed, and acting intelligently and with style, will circumvent unimportant matters and reduce conflicts and counterproductive arguments.

Having covered the key issues of leadership and management, it is time to prepare ourselves for day-to-day conflict in the work place. In part 2, we will discuss safeguards against deceptive thinking, and we will also see the important role style plays in developing the essential tools for effectively deploying such defenses.

PART 2

Safeguards against Deceptive Thinking

5

Clear Thinking

Clear thinking is required to resolve many problems, including many of the practical issues that arise in business and in government. Cautioning against the use of emotional thinking in connection with such issues as trade policy, tax reform, education, health care, immigration, market share, tariffs, and capital investment versus employment, does not mean that emotional thinking has no value. There is a place for emotional thinking, but not where responsible decisions must be made.

Moreover, the frequent use of emotional words is not confined to political thinking. It is common in business also. (And, of course, in social conversation.) But we must be able to thoughtfully disarm our rivals so that the solutions to problems can be carried out effectively, with clear thinking purged of all irrelevant emotion. Impartial investigation of facts divested of irrelevant emotions has given us great advances in the sciences. Such investigation has become more common in business and politics, and its triumphs will be even greater when applied to the most important affairs.

Nevertheless, emotional thinking is rampant; it is everywhere. It really does not matter much if we sometimes use emotional words. We all do, especially when trying to show our conviction. What does matter is that we should not lose the ability to think without using emotional words. Clear thinking (that is, thinking devoid of emotional words) enables us to gain better protection against intellectual exploitation by our unscrupulous rivals. In domestic and international affairs, business as well as politics, ignorance, suspicion, scheming, prejudice, bad manners, and crooked thinking are still prevalent. But many advances toward clear thinking are still possible. We must simply examine human knowledge, conduct, and relationships. Here again, style is key, as clear thinking in our communication style is what will safeguard us against the ploys of deceptive argument.

In the next chapter, we will discuss propaganda and suggestion—and their powerful roles in the workplace environment.

6

Propaganda and Suggestion

Propaganda

What does the word *propaganda* stand for? Propaganda refers to the matter disseminated, or the methods of dissemination used, by people whose deliberate aim is to persuade others to think or do something which they would not otherwise have done or thought. Propaganda is primarily concerned with persuasion, not with the spreading of facts or information. If propaganda provides facts, it does so only with the intention of inducing people to draw particular conclusions from those facts; specifically, conclusions that will make those individuals act in the way the propagandist wants them to act.

Propaganda, as defined above, is not immune to use by the rational and sound-thinking person when he or she seeks agreement on points suggested. It should be employed as often as it makes sense and is beneficial. However, we must avoid misuse of propaganda. We must also always bear in mind that neither orator nor propagandist, private or public, will ever employ judicial impartiality when presenting the pros and cons of any controversial issue. At best, we can scarcely expect propagandists to be much more than special pleaders, selecting and presenting facts in such a way as to put their respective points of view in a favorable light. Propaganda does tend to trade upon the intellectual inertia which besets so many people, and to secure its ends by appealing to their emotions. (This is but one instance of the pitfalls of emotional thinking, as cautioned against in chapter 5.)

There are three ways in which people are apt to derive their opinions from nonrational sources: (1) they tend to think and believe what they wish to think and believe; (2) they allow their feelings to interfere with their interpretation of facts; and (3) they tend to believe what they are told by way of suggestion (i.e., they are suggestible). The propagandist is usually ready to exploit any and all three of these tendencies.

Suggestion

Let's take a closer look at suggestion, the third tendency described above.

The circumstances in which people are most readily suggestible include the following: when they are told something by someone to whom they ascribe prestige; when they are told something in a confident and assured tone; and when a statement is repeated to them again and again. In addition, the more ignorant people are about a topic or an issue, the more suggestible they are likely to be in any of the foregoing circumstances.

Moreover, the state of suggestibility is not as remote from ordinary business life as might be thought. Therefore, we must reserve judgment until we have examined the claims made, and then we must base our judgments on the merits (or lack thereof) that we discover. However, in estimating the value of the evidence gathered during our discovery, we must be careful to remember these key points: (1) time alone does not constitute experience; (2) the experience of the practical man is not necessarily superior to that of the theorist; (3) experience, skill, and/or success in one area does not necessarily warrant a person's speaking with authority on another (in fact, this is an example of false analogy); and (4) repetition and reiteration, however persistent, do not create authority.

To take the third point further, the practical man often cannot see the forest for the trees, and the theorist (i.e., the onlooker) often sees the bigger picture. This is why staff people often see merit in arguing with line management. In addition—and this refers to both the third and fourth points, above—often, the most efficient and successful employee or worker in a limited sphere in any business, industry, or profession, is the very last person to speak with authority on the business as a whole. A successful businessman, merely because he is a successful businessman, is not thereby qualified to express authoritative views on wider issues of economics, much less politics, and vice versa. Yet it happens all the time. In fact, it is very pronounced within companies where, for example, engineers suggest how sales should be run. This is precisely why it is so important to broaden the knowledge bases of top management candidates and thereby despecialize the specialists, as discussed throughout part 1, particularly in chapter 1.

There are many ways in which suggestion conditions an audience or individual listener. Let's examine the circumstances leading to suggestibility, as defined at the start of this section.

First, the effect of prestige will work powerfully, as mentioned previously in this chapter. Simply stated, people are likely to believe those whom they believe to be prestigious. The danger in this lies in the fact that such prestige may or may not be genuine. False credentials are easy enough to obtain, and those who do so use them to acquire unmerited prestige. For example, the well-known trick of using obscure technical jargon in a discussion is often a device for acquiring undeserved prestige. Unfortunately, many people are more easily persuaded by what they cannot or do not understand.

Second, a confident tone and manner significantly aid the success of suggestion. Confidence can be reflected in both posture and speech, particularly a steady, loud voice. An inner feeling of certainty or conviction that the view held is right may be valuable in achieving said confidence, but it is not essential to it. An experienced individual who has learned the trick of the confident manner/tone can put it on like a mask. Many will find it a greater help to their success than any amount of expert knowledge on the aspect of business or government that they are proposing to undertake.

Third, the reliance on repetition or reiteration (repeated affirmation) as a method of suggestion is also effective, but this method must be clearly understood. There are two ways of trying to make somebody else agree with us. One is to put forward honestly the reasons we have for our belief. If we do that, we must be prepared to also consider the other person's reasons for disagreeing with us, and then we must weigh the worth of his or her reasons against our own. Obviously, this is a laborious method, and one that is not likely to lead to a feeling of absolute certainty on the matter in dispute. It has the advantage of being the one method which may help both sides to gain some insight of the truth, however dim that view might be. Such an advantage will not weigh heavily in favor of this method in the minds of those who wish for quick results—who want a feeling of certainty rather than knowledge of truth, and who prefer that people act blindly and enthusiastically under their guidance, rather than deciding calmly and wisely following the presentation of the argument. These individuals opt for another method: that of simply saying over and over again the thing which they want others to believe. This is *repeated affirmation.*

How can merely repeating a statement convince listeners to believe it? That has to be discovered, and as such, it may be described by the term *human suggestibility,* as touched upon earlier. This well-known practice has long been used by those wishing to influence the opinions of others, even when the practitioners have never heard the word *suggestibility.*

In regard to suggestibility, a suggestion is more powerful if in spoken form and not merely in print. The speaker will often repeat himself in different words, partly to avoid monotony and partly to conceal the actual method of persuasion used.

Both propaganda and suggestion illustrate the importance of communication. However, mastering the use of words will be to our benefit only if it goes hand in hand with an attractive and trustworthy appearance. Thus, we come back to style.

Now that we understand how propaganda and suggestion work, let's move on to see the dishonest tricks used in argument, which will be explored in the next chapter.

7

Dishonest Tricks in Argument

In this chapter, we will discuss some dishonest tricks commonly used in argument, along with the methods for overcoming them. (Many of the concepts used in the tricks enumerated here receive more theoretical examination in chapter 6.) The aim here is practical: to win when confronted with crooked thinking in arguments and speeches.

Common Tricks Used in Argument and the Best Safeguards against Them

- **Use of emotionally toned words.** The best safeguard against this is to translate the statement(s) into emotionally neutral words.
- **Diversion to another question or a side issue, or by irrelevant objection.** The best safeguard against this is to refuse to be diverted from the original question; an effective device is to restate the question describing the real issue at hand.
- **Proof by inconsequential argument.** The best safeguard against this is to ask for a clear explanation of the connection between the proposition and the alleged proof, even though the request for explanation may be attributed to ignorance or lack of logical insight on the part of the person making it.

- **Recommendation of a position because it is a mean between two extremes.** The best safeguard against this is to deny the usefulness of this practice as a method for discovering the truth. In practice, this can most easily be done by showing that our own view can also be represented as a mean between two extremes.

- **Begging the question.** The best safeguard against this is to restate our opponent's argument in such a simple way that the nature of this trick will be clear to everyone.

- **Suggestion by repeated affirmation; suggestion by use of confident manner; and suggestion by prestige.** The best safeguard against these tricks that play on suggestibility is to have a theoretical knowledge of the phenomenon of suggestion; if we are aware of the pitfalls of suggestion, it will be easier to detect such ploys when they are used. All three tricks lose much of their effect if the audience sees the way in which the speaker obtains a favorable response to his or her argument. Ridicule is often used to undermine a confident manner, but it will be equally effective to use any kind of criticism that makes the speaker begin to grow angry or plaintive.

- **Prestige by means of false credentials.** The best safeguard against this, when feasible, is to expose the falsity of the schools, degrees, titles, assignments, and so on, that the individual uses.

- **Prestige by use of pseudotechnical jargon.** The best safeguard against this is to ask the speaker to explain him- or herself more simply.

- **The appeal to mundane authority.** The best safeguard against this is to consider whether the person with supposed authority has a sound reason for making the assertion attributed to him or her.

- **Overcoming resistance to a doubtful proposition by preliminary statement of a few easily accepted ones.** The best safeguard against this is simply to have knowledge of this trick so that we are prepared to deal with its effects.

- **Statement of a doubtful proposition in such a way that it fits with the thought habits or prejudices of the listener.** The best safeguard against this is to question what appears to be obvious. A device of particular value against this trick is to restate a questionable proposition in a new context, one in which our individual thought habits do not lead us to automatic acceptance of the proposition in question.

- **Use of ideas generally accepted as *tabloid thinking* as a premise in argument.** There is no truly satisfactory way of dealing with tabloid thinking in argument. The best safeguard against this trick is to point out, with good humor and with the backing of real evidence, that matters are more complicated than our opponent supposes.

- **"There is much to be said on both sides, so I shall make no decision either way"; or any other formula leading to academic detachment from practical life.** The best safeguard against this is to point out that no action has more real, practical consequences than those which result from acting on either of the propositions in dispute, and that this is no more likely than any other to be the right solution for the difficulty at hand.

- **Argument by imperfect analogy.** The best safeguard against this is to examine the alleged analogy in detail, and then to point out where it breaks down.

- **Argument by forced analogy.** The best safeguard against this is to expose the absurdity of the forced analogy, which can best be accomplished by showing how many other analogies supporting different conclusions might have been used.

- **Use of a dilemma that ignores a continuous series of possibilities between two extremes presented.** The best safeguard against this is to refuse to accept either alternative, but instead, to point to the continuity which the person using the argument has ignored. This may be strengthened by pointing out that employing the argument proposed is tantamount to asking if a sheet of paper is black or white when, in fact, it is a shade of gray.

- **Use continuity/similarity in issues to cast doubt on the real difference between them.** The best safeguard against this is to point out that regardless of the similarities, the difference is nevertheless real. Here again, this response can be strengthened by pointing out that application of the same method of argument would deny the difference between *black* and *white* or between *hot* and *cold*.

- **Illegitimate use of, or demand for, definition.** The best safeguard against this is to underscore that the argument at hand is not that simple. In other words, if an opponent uses definitions to produce clear-cut conceptions for facts which are not at all simplistic, it is necessary to point out to him or her how much more complicated the facts are in reality than he or she has implied.

- **Use of ambiguous, vague, or meaningless terms.** The best safeguard against this is to continually demand explanation until the terms become clear; or, to offer such explanation ourselves, asking our opponent if that is what he or she means, and then repeating the argument, with the terms clarified. With a persistently confused thinker, this remedy may be useless; nothing will drive him or her to think clearly. A necessary remedy is to avoid arguing with an opponent who employs this trick.

- **Speculative argument.** The best safeguard against this is to point out that reality cannot be inferred from what ought to be or from what the speaker feels should be.

- **Special pleading.** The best safeguard against this is to apply our opponent's special arguments to other propositions that he or she is unwilling to admit to.

- **Commending or condemning a proposition because of its practical consequences for the listener.** The best safeguard against this is self-awareness. Put differently, we can only become immune to the effect of this kind of appeal if we have formed a habit of recognizing our own tendencies to be guided by our prejudices and by our own self-interest, and also if we have developed a practice of distrusting our own unbiased judgment when faced with issues that impact us personally.

- **Attributing prejudices or ulterior motives to opponents.** The best safeguard against this is to point out that other prejudices may equally well determine the opposite view, and that, in any case, the question of why a person holds an opinion is an entirely separate one from the question of whether that opinion is a right one (which is the question at issue in the first place).

As we have seen throughout our discussion, both straight and crooked thinking have to do with logic. However, logic does not examine how people think; nor does logic examine whether the results of the thinking in question are in tune with reality. (This cannot be decided through thinking alone, but demands the use of other means of knowledge.) All logic does is to examine under which conditions the conclusions based on certain premises are as correct, or as true, as the premises themselves.

It is obvious that all kinds of reasoning and arguments show up in business and politics, and there is no yardstick we can use to always draw the right conclusions from the conditions at hand. We must be able to counteract not only false (mistaken) conclusions but also willful misconstruing; in addition, we also need practical work experience. We cannot afford to make the foolish mistake of supposing that we can settle controversies by attributing prejudices to our colleagues—or our competitors—by labeling their arguments "rationalizations." Our attempt to persevere must be done in a way which will gather the support of others, so the search for the best answer can be done in concert. Again and again, we will come back to the obvious: what we present for approval or acceptance, in terms of positions and views, is much more easily moved forward when backed by a flawless style.

Safeguarding against deception, and overcoming it, is an important skill for success. However, this skill works best in concert with ethical behavior. In part 3, we will more deeply explore the importance of ethics, and we will also see how essential style is in cultivating ethics in our conduct.

PART 3

Ethics

8

Integrity

When we examine the elements which make up class, there is one component that counts as much as the others, if not more: integrity. Integrity is the very basis of class, and both integrity and class are essential to any admirable style. Integrity is also at the heart of ethics. Let's be very clear about this: Nobody can afford *not* to be ethical; if we are not ethical, we put our long-term success rate at risk even, if we manage to get by in present situations, whether our rationale is self-protection or misunderstood deception. Gains based on deception will be erased quite quickly. Having integrity takes courage, and being honest takes courage too. We must be trustworthy, and colleagues and friends should not have to perceive or guess what we mean. Our intended meaning should be readily understandable when we speak; it should make us reliable participants in discussions and activities, and we should be looked upon as loyal to causes as well as people.

There is nothing wrong with being forceful, as long as we assert ourselves with class. There is nothing wrong with standing up for our principles and beliefs, even in the face of strong opposition. Combining straight thinking, good preparation, and effective style in presentation, and showing courage and integrity in all we do, together, will make us motivators. In short, these traits and behaviors create meaningful and lasting relationships, both at work and at home. They build our reputation and establish our style.

To have integrity requires the ability to distinguish between right and wrong, and to apply our principles and values to practical situations. We should not sacrifice our moral principles for short-term, unsustainable gains. Being in the minority, in terms of an issue, is no reason to change our opinion, position, or behavior. More to the point, wrongdoing is never right, even if it reflects the opinions or behavior of the majority. Remember the theory that bad leaders have bad followers. If we feel the views or actions of the majority are wrong, we must have the courage to break the mold; otherwise, our organization or social groups will never make it.

If nothing else, we should be concerned with ethics because behaving ethically is the smart thing to do in all circumstances.

Unfortunately, those who are not ethical may often look like winners—if they are not caught in unethical behavior. As it happens, those who cheat usually get away with it because they have delivered against the objectives. That means we should not concentrate on the status quo, but rather, on how things ought to be. Corporate manuals are not enough. What counts is the personal commitment to doing the right thing, which in turn will establish a framework of reliable conduct. Ethics thus becomes a rule system. Otherwise, conduct which becomes acceptable may not necessarily be proper, and actions which are permitted do not necessarily have to be ethical.

Nevertheless, we often pay a price for being ethical; therefore, ethics is a system which relies on courage, as previously mentioned.

To return to practical terms, let's look at the role of ethics in decision making. We must always ensure that we do not act against existing laws and regulations—the rules, so to speak—and this will necessarily limit our choices, especially if such rules do not reflect ethical behavior or moral courage. To put this another way, playing by the rules is not enough; our conduct must be proper, in terms of ethics and integrity. Taken this way, proper conduct has a narrower definition than it would under the overarching laws and regulations of an organization or government. Essential ethical decisions must support every stakeholder, or at least the majority of stakeholders (e.g., employees or shareholders).

In chapter 1, we discussed certain career issues and the stakes accompanying them. The very pursuit of a career can clearly sacrifice integrity. Be on the lookout for people who want to succeed at any cost, or who adhere to the Managerial Imperative (see chapter 3). Safeguard against such individuals, as their agendas (usually covert) include engaging in cover-ups, concealing facts, sabotaging viable projects, distorting facts, and using such tactics as cheating, blaming, and backstabbing. Despite their inherent dangers, such steps on the career ladder are permitted, and even sanctioned, by many firms. Such organizations either possess a laissez-faire attitude or develop the wrong perception of how to deal with the requirement for immediate results (see parts 1 and 2).

In short, armored with integrity and a convincing style, we will win—not at any cost, but at the right cost.

In the next chapter, we will discuss promise making, the second key component of ethical behavior.

9

Promise Keeping

In both trivial and important matters, we must keep the promises we make. If we doubt that we will be able to keep a promise, we should not make it. Broken promises lead to broken relationships, whether such relationships are at work or in our personal lives.

We must strive to become role models in everything we say and do, and we achieve this by keeping our promises. Similarly, we must also be consistent in what we say and do, and we must treat others with fairness. All this is essential; otherwise what we say and do will cause nothing but confusion. Keeping promises establishes the opposite of confusion, which is reliability.

When we are reliable, as established through keeping our promises, people will expect not only that we will do exactly what we promised to do but also that we will do it in the time frame we promised. Reliability created by repetitive promise keeping instills trust. People rely on the promise maker to keep his or her word and to deliver on commitments. When that happens, the person becomes dependable, which means that colleagues know that the promise maker is a dependable individual who does what he or she promises to do. It also becomes evident that as a dependable person, he or she is well prepared to handle prevailing circumstances. All this makes it difficult for rivals to be deceptive and evasive, because continual dependability and trustworthiness trump deception.

Just as integrity is the basis of class, so is promise keeping the basis of reliability. Both are essential components of the sought-after style that breeds success.

In the next chapter, we will discuss loyalty, the third key component of ethical behavior.

10

Loyalty

Along with integrity and promise keeping, loyalty is a keystone of ethical behavior. Loyalty to the organization and its people is a must if you wish to advance in your career. Such loyalty requires putting ego aside. As a representative of the organization, you must represent it well, stick up for it, and safeguard it. Your colleagues will then trust you and depend on you to do what is right. Loyalty requires two important activities: the first involves looking out for the whole organization and its overall mission, and the second involves looking out for the components of the organization, including the owners (and/or upper management) and the workers.

All that said, keep in mind that loyalty is value based, so be careful when choosing to whom to be loyal—even where management and superiors are concerned. Do not be loyal to a crook, whether your direct supervisor, a member of management, or the owner of the company.

Another important point to remember is that not all information in an organization is made available to everybody. Therefore, the loyalty concept includes being able to be discreet in regard to confidential information, only disseminating it to those who have a need to know and who have been authorized to receive it.

Also, loyalty demands that nobody attempts to circumvent others in order to gain unwarranted benefits, and also that nobody spreads rumors or gossip that could unduly hurt others.

In the end, to put difficult jobs into action without loyalty is nothing but intolerable. Remember that brilliance in work and in style, when combined with loyalty, make it likely that every team member wins.

Now that we've covered three key components of ethical behavior, it's time to learn what not to do, which we will discuss in the next chapter.

11

What Not to Do

Now that we have discussed the key components of ethical behavior—integrity, promise keeping, and loyalty—let's turn our attention to the things we should *not* do when striving for proper conduct and ethics in all our affairs.

First and foremost, do not do anything that you know is wrong, and do not try to rationalize poor behavior with lame excuses. Avoid such responses as "it is not in my job description"; "everybody else does it"; "it's a dumb rule, so I don't have to observe it"; or "I can't afford to be ethical right now." Do not unduly compartmentalize your actions. Do not cheat or lie—which means do not be deceptive in your actions or your speech, and do not take anything that belongs to someone else—or to the company. (Remember Paul Getty, who fired a senior vice president because he took a company stamp and put it on his private letter. Getty's rationale was not only that the senior vice president was a thief but also that the person who takes small things one day may take bigger things at a later time, and, eventually, even do engage in a criminal act.)

The foregoing caveats apply to our behavior outside of work as well as at work. The subsequent items are more specifically related to the workplace. Do not hold back important information from those who need it. Do not do anything merely because it is the popular thing to do, especially when it is clearly wrong. Do not delegate wrongdoing. Do not gossip, especially when it is obvious that it could hurt others. Do not challenge plans agreed upon by management when speaking to subordinates or peers. (Such criticism should go up the organization, if voiced at all.) Do not ignore content; to simply concentrate on developing the mind and not the mind-set will not suffice in truly ethical behavior.

Never attack those who present arguments or proposals; limit your criticism to *what* they present, not to the presenters themselves. Do not express yourself in a way that closes doors. Do not take lightly the perspectives of others, even if disagreeing with them. Do not defend preconceived notions. Do not allow yourself to be forced to make choices which are destructive to you personally or to your organization. Do not procrastinate. Do not think "it cannot happen here." Do not try to receive undeserved rewards. Do not adjust ethical obligations in regard to the conduct of those with whom you interact. Do not assume that good business is good ethics.

Although, as stated, the foregoing paragraph pertains more to business, much of the advice can apply to personal conduct outside of work as well. Here are some caveats that apply to business and life in general. Do not necessarily do what you have the power or desire to do; instead, observe the old rule not doing to others what you wouldn't want others to do to you. Do not underestimate the cost of failing to do the right thing. Do not kill the messenger. Do not intimidate or retaliate; always be fair to those with opposing views.

Finally, in simple terms, we should recognize that the consistency between plans and conduct is a matter of integrity.

We've discussed management and leadership, safeguards against deception, and the importance of ethical behavior. All these are components of impeccable style, to be sure, but having good manners provides the outward display of strong and admirable inner character. Put differently, first impressions speak volumes, and exhibiting good manners enables you to make consistently outstanding first impressions. In part 4, we will take a close look at good manners, the underpinning of style.

PART 4

Good Manners*

---

* The essence of good manners remains fairly uniform through time, but changes do take place. We have compiled data from many sources (beyond the scope of the references section), including ourselves; we have updated the rules and created a limited, commonsense solution. At times, it includes rules with minimal use in contemporary business activities.

12

Tactfulness and Good Manners

Tactfulness and good manners are essential components of proper behavior, both at work and in our personal lives. Adhering to good manners makes human interaction pleasant for everyone. Having good manners is not an issue of birth or rank, but rather of proper training. We each must learn good manners, and then we must exhibit good manners in all circumstances.

The main rule of proper behavior has stood the test of time, and it is the ultimate expression of good manners. It is simply to treat people with consideration and kindness; that said, a good heart will always outweigh formality. This is the true core of admirable style, in the truest sense of the word. As we have said repeatedly, we want to be distinguishable and desirable to be around; conversely, we do not want to be snobbish or overbearing, nor do we want to give the impression of self-importance.

We should not disregard the rules of etiquette if we want to be successful. (We will discuss various points of etiquette in the subsequent chapters of part 4.) However, in our fast-paced society, the niceties of good manners are all too often ignored. It is a mistake to follow behavior that has become frequent by default even though it falls outside the rules of proper conduct. What might be commonplace quite simply is not good enough for those who strive for an admirable style. Put differently, we must have good manners if we want to stand out as exceptional, and that is what style is all about. Furthermore, we must be comfortable and at ease in any situation.

In the subsequent chapters of part 4, we shall cover what professional people will need to know and do in order to display good manners and proper conduct at work and in their personal lives. Often, the rules applicable to business apply equally to social situations, so we will simply address those circumstances we normally face, without attempting to cover the whole field, including such extremes as what to do in the company of royalty. Remember—the higher we climb on the social/corporate ladder, the more important it will be to master the rules of etiquette. By no means are the rules uniform around the world, and so we have included a chapter on traveling abroad so that we can address generally acceptable behavior here at home and internationally, including a few variations that apply in certain foreign countries. It is vital that our good manners be both sensible and in sync with our present time.

Now that we understand the importance of tactfulness and good manners, it's time to move on to the rules of etiquette, which we will cover in the next chapter.

13

Day-to-Day Rules of Etiquette

Greetings

Salutations and Handshakes

- Greater prominence determines who takes the initiative to offer a salutation or handshake.
- Note that in all instances ladies go first when greeting or shaking hands, older people are of greater prominence than younger, and those of more important rank are of greater prominence than those of less important rank.

Kissing

- This custom has strong ties to specific cultures and ethnic backgrounds, and certain rules do apply.
- When kissing on one cheek only, it will usually be the right, or as offered by the lady; do not touch the offered cheek with your lips.
- When kissing on both cheeks, it will be the right one first; again, do not touch the offered cheeks with your lips.

- When kissing a lady on the hand—which is only appropriate for married ladies, and only inside a house or on private property—do not touch the lady's hand with your lips.

Men Hugging Each Other

- If one man takes the initiative, the other man should reciprocate; avoid initiating hugs unless certain the other person will be comfortable.

Presenting (Introducing)

Individuals

- In general, introduce the less important (or less distinguished/prominent) to the more important.
- It is thus appropriate to introduce a gentleman to a lady, a younger person to an older person, and a lower-ranking person to a higher-ranking person.
- Following the introduction itself, if appropriate, add a few personal words.
- Men must be standing when presented; ladies are only required to stand if introduced to prominent persons.
- When introduced to someone, it's best to simply say "good afternoon" or "hello," and then politely smile; avoid responses like "it is a pleasure" or "it is an honor."

Groups

- If presenting to a group, give the presentee's name first, and then name the remaining persons in the group, in the order they stand.
- At a party, first greet the host (and hostess), and then greet others in attendance whom you know.
- If you sit at one among more tables, greet everyone seated at your table.
- The old rules required that it was the job of the hostess to introduce people to each other, while the host's job was to fill the glasses and provide all drinks. In formal circumstances, these rules usually still apply. Under less-formal circumstances, though, the host and hostess can both do the presenting, or people can introduce themselves.
- In airplanes, on trains, on buses, on ferries, and so on, and when traveling in general, it is not necessary to introduce yourself, even if talking to a fellow traveler for hours.

Accompanying

Rank

Highest rank determines the positions of persons:

- the most important (most prominent) person to the right.
- gentlemen always to the left of ladies, except when walking on a narrow sidewalk, where the gentlemen always walk closest to the curb.
- one or more gentlemen never walk in between two ladies.

Here are some examples:

- two gentlemen and a lady walking (left to right, as seen from behind): youngest gentleman, oldest gentleman, the lady (see figure 1).
- two ladies and a gentleman on a sofa (left to right, as seen from behind): gentleman, oldest lady, youngest lady; where 1 is the highest rank and 5 is the lowest, the persons would be seated left to right, as seen from behind: 5-3-1-2-4.

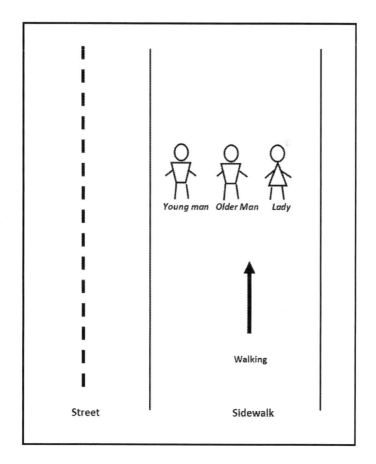

Figure 1

Accompanying. The most important person is on the right, as seen from behind, except when walking on a narrow sidewalk, where the gentleman always walks closest to the curb. Gentlemen walk to the left of ladies, and one or more gentlemen never walk in between two ladies.

Public Greetings

- A gentleman should not stop a lady in the street unless he knows her well.

Staircases

- Down: a gentleman walks slightly behind a lady, leaving her close to the railing.
- Up: a gentleman never walks behind a lady, but next to her; if a steep staircase, a gentleman walks in front of a lady.

Elevators

- A gentleman asks a lady "which floor"; it is exceptionally polite to take her to her floor first, but at least ask the lady her permission to exit before her (these rules are no longer necessary in office buildings or hotels).

Cars

- Ladies sit in the back unless a woman is driving with one lady passenger, who then sits in the front.
- If there are two ladies and two gentlemen in a car, the gentlemen sit in the front.
- Ladies always enter the car from the curb side, after one of the gentlemen has opened the door. A gentleman does not force a lady to move over; he enters from the other side.

- In chauffeur-driven cars, the premier seat is in the back, on the curb side.
- A chauffeur never walks in front of the car; he always goes around the back.

Buses/Trains/Airplanes

- A lady enters first, but she exits after the gentleman so that he can assist her down steep steps.
- On an airplane or train, with or without reserved seats, the gentleman goes first, leading the way.
- When on a full bus or train, it is still nice for a gentleman to offer his seat to a lady; likewise for a younger person to an older.

Restaurants

- A lady enters the restaurant first.
- If no hostess is available, the gentleman walks ahead of the lady, leading the way to the table.
- If hostess is available to escort the guests to their table, the lady always walks in front of the gentleman.
- If a guest arrives early, and it was not decided to meet in the bar, the guest should wait in the entry hall.
- It is not good manners to find the table, sit down, and even worse, order a drink. If the host is late (say, fifteen minutes or more), then the guest may go to the bar and order a drink.
- The host decides the guests' placement at the table. If there is a sofa along the wall, then the lady takes

her place there, and the gentleman sits opposite her. It is quite intimate if he sits next to her. If there are two couples, the ladies should sit on the sofa, opposite the gentlemen; however, spouses should not sit opposite each other. If there is a young and an older couple, the older couple sits on the sofa.

- If the table is a booth, the ladies, the guest of honor, or the oldest person should sit on the inside.
- A gentleman never sits down before a lady, and he always helps her with the chair.
- A gentleman always stands up when a lady comes to sit at the table.
- Friends who come by to say hello are greeted by the gentleman, who stands up; ladies remain sitting.
- The host orders food and drinks for the guests; a guest should not choose unless asked by the host.
- If the host orders coffee after the main course, it should be clear that he does not want dessert served; a guest should therefore not ask for it.
- In many places around the world, it is not in good taste to discuss business during the meal—at least not until coffee is served.
- Always treat the staff politely, but do not enter into lengthy conversations with them, particularly not at business functions.
- The host should not complain loudly about the food or the service; if it is not good, just don't come back.
- At time of payment, there is nothing wrong with going over the check, preferable at an empty table; in any case, be discreet.

- When leaving a restaurant, the lady goes out first, and the gentleman takes care to help her with her coat before he puts on his own.

Theaters

- A gentleman enters a row in front of a lady, but then all ladies enter before the next gentleman.
- Going down a row, you face those you pass—never turn your back to them, as this is not only odd but also impolite.

Lining Up

- Lining up (or queuing) is based on ancient Roman law, where the one who is first in time, is first in right (also known as first come, first served).

Proper Attire

General Rules

- Ladies' dress code follows that of gentlemen; on invitations to formal occasions, the gentlemen's dress requirement is indicated.
- It's preferable to underdress than overdress, especially during the day. (Never look like you tried too hard.)
- It's better to have a few garments of high quality than more garments of lesser quality.

Blazers

- For informal occasions, blazers should be black or blue, and worn with charcoal, gray, or beige pants.
- A tie is not necessary (if informal).
- The badge on the breast pocket should not be garish or boastful.
- Brass buttons are fine, particularly if they express association with an esteemed club or group.
- Sleeve buttons should have real buttonholes.

Business Attire

The rules below may be relaxed locally, but they still apply in general.

Gentlemen

- Suits should be dark (black or blue) or gray.
- Suits with pattern or stripes should not be garish.
- Double-breasted or single-breasted are equally fine; never wear a double-breasted jacket open, and always leave the lowest button unbuttoned; a single-breasted jacket may be left unbuttoned, but that is not preferable; no vest with double-breasted; vest with single-breasted may look outdated (if used, leave the lowest button unbuttoned); vest is always in the same fabric as the suit.

- Shirts should preferably be white, with French cuffs, but definitely a light, neutral color (never wear a pink shirt); do not wear a striped shirt with striped suit; if wearing a long-sleeve shirt (jacket off), cuffs may be rolled up, but only twice, and never above the elbow.

- Ties may be somewhat loud, if tasteful; do not wear a striped tie with a striped shirt or a striped suit; a tie should reach to the waist in order to avoid a gap between the waistband of the pants and the bottom of the tie; do not wear a bow tie.

- Handkerchiefs are a nice touch, and white is always a good color; colors other than white should accent the most discreet color in the tie; try not to wear tie and handkerchief in the same design and color; the handkerchief can be placed in the breast pocket in any of the following ways: (1) insert the center of the handkerchief first, leaving the corners visible; (2) place the center of the handkerchief over your fist and then press the center into your fist, gather the corners along the portion inserted into your fist, and place the handkerchief in your pocket; (3) place the handkerchief with a straight line visible across the pocket.

- Shoes should preferably be black leather (never patent leather); if wearing brown shoes, they should be dark, but never worn with black or blue suits; also, brown shoes are not to be worn after six in the evening.

Ladies

- Appropriate business attire for ladies includes dresses, suits, skirts or slacks, and blouses or sweaters can be worn with the suits, skirts, or slacks.
- How you dress for work is important, since it is a direct reflection of how you see yourself.
- You should always dress for the position you want, not necessarily the position you are in.
- Clothes that are obscenely tight or revealing are not appropriate.
- For business-oriented social events in the evening, long dresses may be appropriate; follow the dress code listed on the invitation. (See "general rules," at the beginning of this section.)

Tuxedo (Dinner Jacket, Black Tie)

- Invitations stating "Black tie" require gentlemen to wear a tuxedo; ladies follow the gentlemen's stated dress code (see below).
- With a tuxedo, wear a white shirt (may be plain) with French cuffs, black bow tie (or same color as vest), and lacquered shoes.
- The tuxedo should preferably be black or midnight blue.
- In the summer, white dinner jackets with dark pants is acceptable attire.

- The tuxedo may be single-breasted or double-breasted; a vest or cummerbund is not worn with a double-breasted tuxedo.
- Do not wear a belt with a tuxedo; suspenders, if used, should be narrow, and white, black or dark blue all are acceptable.
- A tuxedo should not be worn before five in the evening; therefore, it is really not correct to wear a tuxedo at many morning/afternoon church weddings.
- Ladies may wear long or short dresses (both may be sleeveless) for private black-tie parties; skirts or dress pants, with fancy blouses may also be worn.

Tailcoat (White Tie)

- Invitations stating "Formal" require gentlemen to wear a tailcoat; ladies follow the gentlemen's stated dress code (see below).
- With a tailcoat, wear a white shirt, a white tie, and a white vest (all buttons must be buttoned).
- Never wear a wristwatch with tailcoat.
- Only wear civil dress to a formal affair; decorations (medals) may be worn without being prescribed on the invitation.
- Ladies wear long dresses and long white gloves (never eat with gloves on).
- A tailcoat is mandatory for afternoon weddings (three o'clock or later) if no dress code is indicated on invitation (since this rule is not widely known, it is advisable to note the dress code on the invitation).

Morning Coat (City Dress)

- Morning coats are not used very much.
- Wear a black vest (unless a morning wedding [before three o'clock] and subsequent lunch, in which case the vest is gray).

Jewelry

- Gentlemen wear very little jewelry; any jewelry worn should be for utility, not ornament; do not wear any diamonds, and, besides a wedding band, school ring, and possibly a signet ring on the little finger, do not wear any rings.
- Ladies do not traditionally wear diamonds and pearls before noon (but this is an old rule which may be discarded).
- Gentlemen's watches should preferably be gold (white or yellow); opt for tastefulness; a gold band is not necessary, as leather or crocodile suffices very well.
- Ladies' watches may have diamond ornaments.
- Smart watches are fine to wear, of course.
- Rings should not be worn on the index finger or the middle finger (again, there is no reason to follow this rule literally).
- Studs should be white pearl, gold, or black onyx.
- Cuff links should be understated; too large is not elegant.
- Ladies should not wear ankle chains.

Emblems

- In business, it does not make sense to wear them, since they often indicate political or other preferences which may be offensive to a customer or a prospect.

Hats

- Hats are not commonly worn, but ladies may wear them to lunch, exhibitions, and weddings; hats are never worn in theaters or at dinner; ladies keep their hats on inside the house.
- Gentlemen always remove their hats on entering a house, but may keep them on in public areas of buildings (but not in elevators); when meeting a female acquaintance, either in the street or at a public gathering, it is not necessary for a gentleman to remove his hat, but he touches it as a mark of respect.

Purses and Briefcases

- Should be left in the entry hall or in a corner of the room; if they are very small, it is acceptable to leave them on the chair or in your lap—never on the table.

Overcoats

- Wool and lamb's wool are preferred for overcoats.
- Gentleman should not wear black or dark-blue raincoats.
- Beige is acceptable.

Gloves

- If worn outside, ladies keep their gloves on when shaking hands; gentlemen do not.

Having covered the basic rules of etiquette, let's extend those rules to the sphere of parties and entertaining, the topic of the next chapter.

14

Rules of Etiquette for Parties and Entertaining

Invitations and RSVPs

- Written invitations and responses to them (RSVPs; see below) are done in the third person, which does not require a signature.
- Invitations to small parties are often done by telephone, as are the RSVPs.
- Written invitations should indicate the special occasion for the party.
- The invitation should always state the gentleman's dress requirement (the lady then knows what to wear [see "proper attire," chapter 13]), e.g., "Informal," "Formal," or "Black tie," unless the invitation is for lunch or an open house, in which case no dress code is stated.
- The address is written in the lower left-hand corner.
- "RSVP" (*répondez s'il vous plaît,* meaning "please reply") appears in the lower right-hand corner; the RSVP requires a response, or "Regrets only," meaning that it is only necessary to respond if unable to come.

- If a married couple is invited, and the key person, whether the husband or wife, is unable to attend, they will send their regrets; if the least important of the two is unable to attend, the other one may still attend, and when responding, may apologize that the spouse will not be able to come. (For smaller parties, it is polite to telephone first to ask whether it will be acceptable to come alone.)

- The invitation may have "Regrets only" crossed out, and instead, there may be a handwritten "P.M." (*pro memoria* or *pour memoire*; meaning, "as a reminder").

- Using "P.M." means that the guest has been invited by telephone and has accepted; therefore, a response to the invitation is not required.

- In replying to an invitation (within two days is preferable, but two weeks before the party, at the latest), a handwritten response is preferable, but a response by telephone can be acceptable if the host/hostess is a friend; in business, the secretary may respond, using the title of the person invited (in contrast to the handwritten reply, which uses the invited person's given name).

- Do not be too short and abrupt in declining an invitation.

- It is in bad taste to cancel an invitation after initially having accepted it, and it is unforgivable to do so shortly before or on the same day as the party.

Arriving for the Party

- Do not arrive early (ahead of the time stated on the invitation).
- It's fine to arrive exactly on time and to count on a margin of up to a half hour for a large party; if that cannot be accommodated, should call and apologize for the late arrival. (If the invitation states 7:35 p.m., that could mean it is important for all to arrive on time, since the guest of honor always arrives last. In some countries, like England, 8:30 p.m. is a precise time, so do not arrive at 8:29 p.m. or at 8:31 p.m.)

Bringing Gifts to the Party

- It is not necessary to bring a gift, especially on return visits; bringing a gift is uncommon in many countries.
- Nice gifts for the host/hostess include chocolate, books, wine, and flowers (though it's better to send flowers in advance or on the day after the party, with a thank-you note).
- If bringing a gift, enclose a visiting card and handwrite a short personal note on it.
- When having a large party, place gifts on a special table, and open them after dinner; it is impolite not to open them during the party.
- At small parties, open gifts as the guests arrive.

Conversation at the Party

- There are no longer taboo topics for conversations at formal parties; everything can be discussed, preferably topics of interest to the listeners—just make the conversation pleasant and interesting. (Formerly, taboo topics included politics, dogs, sex, illness, servants, money, food, and many others.)

- It is acceptable to talk about yourself, as long as it doesn't dominate the conversation.

- Show interest in others' opinions, and be considerate to all.

- Ask questions instead of only making statements.

- Do not forget to make genuine compliments and expressions of flattery.

- At dinner, a gentleman should talk mostly with his companion, but should also spend considerable time conversing with the lady on his other side (see figure 2).

- Be silent about the negative; make your companion bloom, not fade.

- At smaller parties or groupings (half a dozen to a dozen), it is preferable to include as many as possible in a conversation, instead of having them one-on-one.

- When speaking to prominent persons, do not use informal terms, such as *you* and *your,* without preceding them with the person's name or title (e.g., "Mrs. Jones, would you like to join me in the garden?" Not "Would you like to join me in the garden?").

Smoking at the Party

- With all the recent restrictions on smoking in public (and in the workplace), it may be better to simply not smoke, even when at private functions; similar considerations are applicable at the dinner table.
- If with a group of nonsmokers, ask for their permission before you smoke.
- If you do smoke, wait until after the main course, or even better, until coffee is served, but only if there are ashtrays on the table.
- Before lighting a cigarette, always offer cigarettes to others, preferably from a case; if from a pack, push one or two cigarettes out, just a little, so they are easy to take.
- A gentleman should always strike the match toward himself.
- A lady should never light a cigarette for a gentleman, but she can hand him a lighter or some matches; neither should she blow out the flame after her cigarette is lit.
- Because of superstition, never light three cigarettes with the same match.
- Never talk with a cigarette hanging in your mouth.
- Never put out cigarettes or cigars on plates, and never leave a lit one in an ashtray.

The above rules of etiquette apply to all sorts of parties. In the pages that follow, we will discuss the specific rules for cocktail parties and dinner parties, respectively.

Cocktail Parties

- May take place in a club, at a restaurant, or at home.
- The receiving line is the following: first the host, then guest of honor and his or her spouse (or significant other), and then the hostess.
- If there is no servant, the host should make and serve the drinks (therefore, there is no real receiving line).
- Cocktail parties normally last two to three hours, between 5:00 p.m. and 8:00 p.m. (e.g., 5:30 p.m. to 7:30 p.m.).
- Do not stay beyond the time given on the invitation.
- The host or hostess should not ask certain guests to stay for dinner after the cocktail party.
- At larger parties, one or more bars are necessary, along with plenty of waiters and waitresses to serve drinks from trays; if canapés are served, there should be one kind per tray, but several kinds on the various trays, to fit a variety of tastes.
- Circulation is important; do not stay in groups of colleagues, or stick to an acquaintance or spouse; do not follow Parkinson's theory on circulation at cocktail parties, according to which, guests circulate left around the room by the walls, thereby avoiding the important guests who congregate in the middle.
- Do not constantly search out other people by looking around, instead of looking at the person you are speaking with, even if he or she is not prominent or of high rank; such looking away

from your conversation partner is very rude and embarrassing. (A cocktail party must not be used as a trade-off for a dinner invitation owed to someone.)

- Dress is a business suit (ladies are no longer required to wear hats); if going to a dinner party after the cocktail party, a tuxedo may be worn.
- When leaving, thank the hostess (and possibly the host), but if she is busy, it is better to leave without interrupting to say good-bye.
- It is not necessary to send a thank-you note after a cocktail party; it is sufficient to call.

Dinner Parties

Welcome Drinks

- Cocktails, and to a lesser degree, fortified wine and aperitifs are common before dinner, even though many wine experts consider it wasteful.
- The welcome drink may be the same as the one guests start with at the dinner table; for example, sherry or champagne.
- It is unnecessary to serve anything with welcome drinks; do not serve chips and dips with welcome drinks, but nuts and olives are acceptable.
- It is better to serve welcome drinks from trays instead of from a bar; no more than one or two glasses per person.

Entering the Dining Room to Start the Meal

- The host enters first (with his companion), and the hostess (with her escort) enters last.
- The hostess sits down first, and the host sits down last.
- Ladies sit down before gentlemen.
- The hostess takes her napkin and places it in her lap, which is the sign that everyone else can do so.
- The hostess starts to eat first (no one else may begin to eat before she does).

Table Plan

- For bigger parties, it is preferable to write down the seating arrangement and place it in the entry hall (this makes it easier for the couple to find each other during the welcome drinks).
- Often, there is no written table plan; everybody scans name cards on the table.
- The host and hostess sit at each end of table; or, routinely, across from each other on each side of the center of the table.
- The hostess has the party's oldest or most prominent gentleman at her right side; on her side of the table, all gentlemen shall be seated with their companions to their left (see figure 2).
- The host has the oldest or the most esteemed lady (or a lady who has not previously been to the house) at his right side; all ladies on the host's side of the table are seated to the right of their escorts (see figure 2).

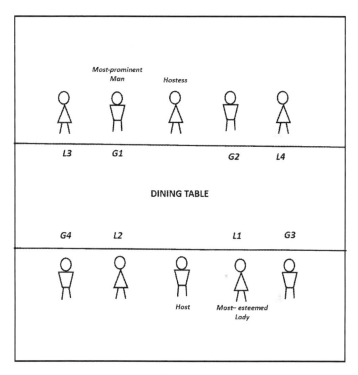

Figure 2

Table Plan. Basic rule is that a gentleman's companion is seated to his left. Try to avoid married couples sitting across from each other; on the host's side of the table, the seating can be reversed so ladies are seated to the right of their escorts. Gentlemen are indicated with G1, G2, G3, and G4; ladies are indicated with L1, L2, L3, and L4—in all instances, the lowest number is the highest rank or family seniority. Host and hostess sitting at each end of the table separates the most-prominent persons.

- The host and hostess must not take each of the same married couple at their sides.
- At many small private parties, the guests may be placed in accordance to background, language proficiency, and age.
- If there is only one lady at the party—the hostess— she shall be seated to the left of the guest of honor; the guest of honor may also be seated to the right of the host.
- If all the guests are ladies, the hostess has the guest of honor on her left or opposite her.
- At parties where all the guests are gentlemen, the host shall have the guest of honor at his right side or opposite him.
- Engaged couples should sit together; married couples never sit together.
- If several tables are used, make sure no table appears more prominent than any other; at each table, there should be a lady or gentleman of the host's nationality or family who can act as the hostess or host of that table.

Table Setting

- Endless courses and a long row of wineglasses are not necessary; in fact, such a setting could easily be perceived as newly rich.
- Here a little history may serve as a good illustration. During the latter part of the nineteenth century, it became custom in England to use a separate set of

knives and forks for each course, whereas Americans and Europeans may still use the same knife and fork for all the courses (except dessert). To avoid messing up the tablecloth, cutlery rests may be used when plates are changed.

- The components of the table setting appear below.

Cutlery

Below is the layout of cutlery, in order of use:

- Knives and soupspoon (larger than the dessert spoon) go to the right of plate(s) (blades toward plate).
- Forks are at the left, with the butter knife at the right of the bread plate.
- If a fish knife (also a nineteenth-century custom) is not used, use a fork or knife instead.
- Dessert spoon, fork, and knife are all placed above place setting; there is no need to worry about which piece of dessert cutlery is to be placed with handles to the left—simply place all with handles to the right.
- Dessert cutlery may not be placed until dessert is to be served.
- Dessert knives are used exclusively for cheese (see figure 3) and fruit.
- Dessert spoons are only used when absolutely necessary, such as for strawberries with cream.

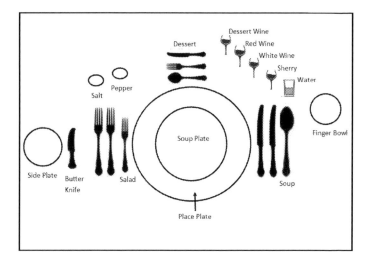

Figure 3

Table Setting. Here is an illustration of a formal table setting with the correct placement of the various pieces. You may not ordinarily go to this extent, but it gives the basis for easily deciding on simpler settings.

Plates

- A place plate may be used; metal is a good choice.
- A dinner plate (main course) may also be used as a place plate.
- The bread plate is at the far left.
- The finger bowl is at the far right.

Glasses

- Glasses are placed on an angle, to the right of the plates, in order of use from right to left.
- If used, the water glass (preferably without a stem) is at the right.
- Beer glass goes to the left of any water glass; no beer with wine or at formal dinners.
- Never use colored glasses.
- Glasses for white and red wine should neither be too big nor too small (about ten ounces); a glass which closes a bit at the top is preferable; the foot and stem should be round and a little shorter than the cup; tulip-shaped champagne glasses are the most widely used (between four and seven ounces), but if you don't have them, just use regular wineglasses; port and sherry are best served in smaller glasses.

Tablecloth

- Tablecloths should preferably be white.
- Even at more formal settings, place mats are acceptable.

Napkins

- Napkins should preferably be white.
- Fold and place napkin on the center of the plate.
- Restaurants sometimes fold the napkin in the shape of a swan or some other form; do not do that when entertaining at home.
- Never place a napkin in a glass.
- If temporarily leaving the table, place your napkin on your chair.
- After dinner, fold your napkin loosely and place it at the left of your place setting.

Ashtrays

- If allowing smoking at the party, ashtrays should be placed on the table just before a pause, if any, after the main course.

Menu

- The date appears on top, then the courses, and, at bottom, the wines.

- The menu is placed at the right of the place plate, above the knives.

Finger Bowls

- Finger bowls are placed at the right of the place setting.

Wine Bottles

- It's best not to place wine bottles on the table, whether full or empty; bottles belong on a serving table.
- If placed on the table (i.e., at an informal party), use bottle trays.
- Carafes may be placed on the table.

Bread Plate

- The bread plate is placed at left side of place setting.
- The bread plate may also be used for salad.
- If there is no bread plate, it is acceptable to put an unbuttered piece of bread or roll on the tablecloth.

Name Cards

- Place name cards on top of the highest glass.
- Name cards must always be handwritten.
- When you sit down, after placing the napkin in your lap, remove the name card; place the name card above the place setting.

- For gentlemen, use only the last name and title, or the first name and last name (without *Mr.* in front).
- For ladies, use *Mrs.*, *Miss,* or their respective heraldic titles.
- For persons in prominent positions, the professional title can be used without the name (e.g., *Secretary of Defense, Ambassador to France,* etc.).

Serving

- It's essential to follow the rule, which is to serve on the left when guests help themselves to food from a tray or when the food is brought to their plates, and serve on the right for food which is placed before the guests, such as a deep plate with soup or a plate with the main course.
- When using serving trays, it's more elegant to allow guests to help themselves to the food than to serve them.
- Wines, beer, and liquor are poured on the right side.
- Do not use a wine-serving holder at the dinner table.
- (Vintage) port is served from right to left around the table; the host is served first.
- Plates are placed and removed from the right side; if a used plate is removed at the same time that a new plate is placed, the used plate is removed from the left, and the new one is placed from the right (this requires extra staff).

- Do not start removing plates until everybody has finished the course (at restaurants, tell wait staff in advance).

- The staff serves the most prominent lady (at the host's right side) first, then the lady at the host's left side, and then continues to the left; the host is served last.

- The main course, and possibly the dessert course, is served twice when from a tray; and the hostess is served first during the second round (to encourage others to take more).

- Servers should never offer cutlery by hand, but always from a plate (e.g., when in replacement for a piece cutlery that has fallen on the floor).

- If coffee (or tea) is poured in a cup and then served (on the saucer, of course), it must be served on the left side; when cream and sugar are on the tray with the cups, the guest uses these condiments before taking the cup from the tray.

- When a guest is served, he or she should always take the closest cake, glass, piece of meat, and so forth.

- Tea can be served as is, with lemon or milk; if using milk, tea should always be poured after adding sugar and/or milk (never use cream in tea, and never use tea bags).

- If cakes (such as pastries) are served at tea, it is preferable to serve all the same kind.

Wines

- Always follow the general rule, which is to serve from light to heavy, with no sweet wines except for dessert.
- If soup is served, it's fine to start with sherry or dry champagne.
- Dry white wine is good for fish, shellfish, and light hors d'oeuvres (red wine can taste fine with fish).
- Serve red Bordeaux for light meat courses; burgundy or Rhône wine for beef and game.
- Do not drink wine with yellow asparagus or with salad that has a vinegar marinade.
- Before serving dessert, the table is cleared of everything (except wineglasses) having nothing to do with dessert, such as salt and pepper, knives, forks, bread plates, and so forth.
- With cheese, serve burgundy or port.
- With fruit, no wine is served (it's fine to serve water).
- With cakes and sweet desserts, serve sweet sauternes, port, or sweet champagne.
- Wineglasses remain on the table during the whole dinner.
- If cognac or liqueurs are offered with coffee, guests choose from what is offered and do not ask for something else.
- The host is served wine first (only a little bit); when he approves, the wine is served to his companion, and then his glass is filled, as are all glasses around the table.
- Wine is always served with the food it accompanies.

Serving Temperature for Wine, Beer, and Liquor

- Always remember that colder is not better, and do not ever add ice cubes.
- Serve white wines and champagne from the refrigerator or at a slightly higher temperature; it's better to place white wines and champagne in a cooler with ice and water.
- Serve red wines at room temperature or slightly cooler; except for burgundy, which is served cellar cold.
- Decant old wines only to get rid of sediments, and even then, only just before drinking.
- Serve cordials and fortified wines (such as port and sherry) at room temperature.
- Serve beer from the refrigerator or at a slightly higher temperature.

Filling the Glasses

- Sherry glasses are filled three-quarters full.
- Wineglasses (white wine) are filled half full.
- Wineglasses (red wine) are filled slightly more than half full.
- Water glasses are filled three-quarters full.
- Beer glasses are filled three-quarters to full (do not pour the beer into a tilted glass).
- Port glasses are filled two-thirds full.
- Champagne glasses are filled to almost full.
- Cognac glasses are filled less than one-quarter full.

Dinner Speeches and Toasts

Speeches

- Two speeches are obligatory at large parties: at the beginning, the host welcomes the guests, and may or may not name the toastmaster or master of ceremony; at the end, the hostess's escort addresses the hostess (her escort is the only speaker who should compliment the food).
- If a guest of honor is present, the first speech after the welcome speech must be for him or her; this and other speeches should not take place before completing the main course.
- At large formal dinners, besides the two obligatory speeches, the host's main speech for the guest of honor and the guest of honor's speech during dessert should be the only speeches.
- If several speeches take place, the sequence is in accordance with the guests' ranking, which is determined by age and closeness to the guest of honor (oldest person and person closest to the guest of honor speak first).
- The other guests should not talk, eat, or drink during a speech (and servants should not move around).

Toasts

- The host makes the first toast at dinner.
- With a lady at his left, a gentleman holds the glass in his right hand; with a lady at his right, he holds the glass in his left hand.
- Wineglasses should be lifted at the top of the stem, with the fingers touching the bottom of the cup, or bowl, of the glass; never hold the wineglass by the middle of the stem or by the cup itself.
- When offered a toast, use the same wineglass that the person toasting is using.
- When toasting, lift the glass slightly above the middle of your chest.
- Do not toast with a water glass at formal dinners.
- Do not "bottom up" (chug or swig) when toasting.
- Do not ever toast with an empty glass.
- Do not touch glasses against each other at a formal dinner.
- A gentleman toasts his wife's escort at the table.
- A gentleman also always toasts his wife.
- The old rule of returning a toast within three minutes is no longer necessary.
- Do not offer a toast to the hostess at large, formal dinners.
- It is the host's duty to toast the male guests and the oldest among the ladies.
- At informal occasions, it's fine to toast anybody.

Table Manners

- Preferably, use the internationally accepted etiquette for holding a fork and knife: fork in the left hand and knife in the right hand at all times.
- Take only one food at a time on the fork, and, as appropriate, use the back side of the fork.
- Do not rest elbows or forearms on the table when eating.
- Never place cutlery you are using on anything but the plate (for example, iced-tea spoons must be removed after stirring; it is correct to serve the iced-tea glass on the plate where the spoon is to be placed, never on the table).
- If you have not finished eating but need to put down your knife and fork, place them on the plate (never on the table and touching the plate), at four and eight o'clock, with the fork's teeth against the plate.
- Place cutlery (fork's teeth upward) on the plate after use, either parallel to the edge of the table (handles to the right) or at a ninety-degree angle to the edge of the table (handles toward the edge).
- Do not blow on hot food; wait for it to cool down.
- Do not reach for food, salt, and so on; ask for the items you require.
- Do not talk with any food in your mouth.
- Do not chew with your mouth open, and do not smack your lips.

- Do not bring your head toward the food; take the food to your mouth.
- Do not bring food directly from the tray to your mouth; place all food on your plate before eating it.
- Do not eat too fast.
- Never use bread to push food onto your fork.
- Do not use toothpicks.
- Do not dip anything in coffee, tea, milk, and the like.
- Sugar cubes may be taken with your fingers.
- Never spit out any food; if you have too-hot food in your mouth, drink water.
- Use a fork or spoon to bring such items as cherry pits from your mouth to your plate, as appropriate.
- Small fish bones may be taken from your mouth to your plate with your fingers.
- Do not use your own knife, fork, or spoon for mustard jars, salt cups, jams, and so on.
- Butter from the butter serving plate is taken with a butter knife (if no butter knife, use your own knife) to your own bread plate; use your own knife to put the butter on the bread.
- Break bread (do not cut it with a knife) one piece at a time when ready to eat it, and then add butter if desired.
- Oysters must not be cut; they are eaten whole (flesh of the oyster only, from the shell).
- Fill soupspoon away from yourself.
- Do not lift your plate to get the last of the soup (in some countries, including the United States, this is

acceptable, but only if lifting the plate away from yourself).

- Never leave your spoon in your cup (soup or coffee); if a soup plate (deep plate) is used, the spoon must be left on the plate.

- If a soup cup has two handles, and the soup is clear and light, it is permissible to drink from the cup, using both handles, but not until half the soup has been consumed.

- Soup-cup lids are to be placed on the cover plate to avoid dripping on the tablecloth; put the lid back on the cup when finished with the soup.

- Do not cut food in advance of eating it; cut and eat one piece at a time.

- Do not use your fingers unless eating yellow asparagus, artichokes, frog legs, corn on the cob, and shellfish (lobster, crab, shrimp, and so on), and chicken legs or ribs when served for lunch.

- Salad may be served separately, often before main course; or it may be served on the bread plate together with, or right after, the main course, which is not common in this country (as opposed to Europe and other places [see chapter 16]).

- Salad should be eaten and cut with a fork only; never cut salad with a knife.

- Do not pick grapes one by one; use a grape scissors or break off the stem.

- Do not eat cheese with a knife and fork; when served, cut from the cheese(s) you choose, and place the pieces you cut on your plate; break off a piece of bread, cut a little piece of the cheese on your plate, and put the piece of cheese on the bread, which you may then eat with your fingers.

- Do not eat dessert with spoon unless it is liquid; even ice cream should be eaten with a fork, unless it is served with a sauce, in which case a fork or spoon may be used.

- Use a fork for soft cakes; dry cakes are eaten with the fingers.

- Any cake in paper cups must not be removed from the paper when offered; take the whole thing on your plate, after which the cake is taken out of the paper and eaten with the fingers, or possibly with a fork.

- Dessert chocolate is eaten with the fingers; as with cakes, if in paper, take the chocolate to your plate or into your hand; when chocolate is offered, take the smallest piece closest to you.

- When drinking coffee at a table, leave the saucer on the table.

- Never use the coffee spoon to get the remaining sugar at the bottom of the cup.

- When coffee is being refilled, do not hand the cup alone, but on the saucer.

- Never use a spoon to sip coffee or tea; the spoon for coffee and tea is used for stirring—when finished using the spoon, put it back on the saucer.

- If you bring food or wine to a party, do not leave with what is leftover.

Finishing Dinner and Leaving the Dining Room

- The hostess should finish eating last.
- The hostess and her escort are the first to leave the table after dinner.
- The other guests follow the hostess and her escort.
- The host and his companion are the last to leave.

After-Dinner Coffee

- It is the easiest to serve the coffee at the dinner table, as opposed to the living room or outside (weather permitting).
- Some do follow the old rule that says the gentlemen are to remain in the dining room for up to an hour after dinner to discuss business, politics, sports, and so on; the host then suggests joining the ladies in the living room at the appropriate time.
- When coffee is served in the living room, the cups (on saucers) may be placed on low tables, or they may be served from trays or from a special serving table where the guests help themselves.
- If the guests are standing when being served coffee, there is better opportunity for the guests to circulate.
- At large parties, a gentleman stays with his companion during coffee, whereas at small parties it is perfectly all right for him to leave his dinner companion so that both can mix with other guests before and during coffee.

- The rules for socializing are the same as for cocktail parties; spouses should not stay together or in the same grouping, or the same room, if possible.

Recap of Some Rules about Coffee

- If standing, hold the cup (and saucer) in your left hand.
- If sugar and cream are served with the coffee from a tray, help yourself to it before taking the cup and saucer.
- Using your fingers to take sugar cubes is acceptable.
- Never leave the spoon in the cup; place the spoon on the saucer.
- When at a table where coffee is served, always hand over the cup on the saucer; never hand over the cup by itself.
- At tables, leave the saucer on the table when drinking the coffee, and only take one sip when bringing the cup to your mouth.
- Do not use the coffee spoon to sip the coffee or to get the sugar from the bottom of the cup.
- Even if dessert was served at the dinner table, most people like some chocolates, petit fours, or biscuits with the coffee when it is served in the living room.

Dancing

- These days dancing at dinner parties is not at all as common as it once was; nevertheless, let's not ignore the basic rules.
- A gentleman dances first with his companion at the table, and then with his wife; next, he invites the lady sitting on his other side to dance with him, and then he asks the hostess to dance; after these compulsory dances, it is open selection.
- A gentleman asks a lady's escort for permission to dance with her.
- It is considerate for a gentleman to pay attention to those ladies who are not dancing, and then to ask them to dance.
- A young gentleman should dance with the daughter of the house at least once, and also with some of the other young girls.
- Nowadays it is acceptable for a lady to ask a gentleman to dance.
- It is impolite to dance with the same partner the whole evening; maximum three dances in a row with the same partner.
- A lady should only reject an invitation to dance if she can give a polite and acceptable reason.
- A gentlemen should never leave a lady alone in order to dance with someone else.

Leaving a Party

- Say good-bye wherever the party has ended (e.g., in the living room), not at the main entrance door, and do so before putting on your overcoat.
- Do not leave before the guest of honor or the oldest or highest-ranking guest has left, unless it is absolutely necessary.
- When at a business dinner, you should normally not stay beyond two and a half to three and a half hours.

Expressing Thanks

- After having been to a party, you should call or write the host and hostess the next day (but no later than within three days).
- It is always nice to send a small bouquet of flowers with a thank-you note.

Armed with the rules of etiquette, both basic and specific to parties and such, let's move on to the finer points of good manners in our communications. In the next chapter, we will discuss visiting cards and telephone etiquette.

15

Visiting Cards and Telephoning

Visiting Cards

- Use first-class paper (white or pale yellow).
- Do not use cards with rounded corners.
- Use engraved cards or plain printing before using embossed cards.
- State your name, title, address, and the like, on business cards.
- Keep it classic; anything else is vulgar.
- Business people traveling abroad should get cards in the appropriate foreign language(s).
- On private cards (as opposed to business cards), put the name only (a gentleman puts *Mr.* in front of his name), possibly with the name of city.
- Business cards are not to be used privately.
- An unmarried woman puts only her first name and family name on the card.
- A married woman does not use her own first name, but her husband's first name (e.g., *Mrs. John Doe*).
- Notations on a visiting card are done above the name; if more space is needed, start below the name, and continue on the back side.

- You never sign a visiting card; for good friends, cross out the family name.
- It is no longer popular to pay visits (which are no longer than fifteen minutes), but if paying a visit, call in advance to ask whether it is convenient to stop by for a moment.
- It is still correct to use abbreviations in French and write them in the lower left-hand corner of the card; some common abbreviations include "P.R." (*pour remercier* [to thank]); "P.C." (*pour condoler* [to express condolences]); "P.F." (*pour féliciter* [to congratulate]); "P.P." (*pour présenter* [to present/introduce]); "P.P.C." (*pour prendre congé* [to say farewell, to take leave of]).
- If the card is delivered personally, it is bent on the left side along the full length of the card.

Telephoning

- Answer by saying the telephone number or the last name of the owner of the residence (possibly also the first name).
- The person telephoning shall introduce him- or herself by stating his or her first and last name.
- If disconnected, the one who called calls again.
- The one who calls also ends the conversation.
- If you have visitors, do not answer the phone.
- When in the company of others, do not answer a cell (mobile) phone.

- Ordinarily, do not have someone call for you; especially if you are subordinate to or younger than the person you are calling, or if you want to ask a favor.
- If you do not call yourself, make sure you are available as soon as the connection has been made to the other line.
- If a secretary calls, he or she should say, for example, "Is this Mr. Davenport? ... Just a moment ... Mr. Jones would like to speak with you."
- A secretary should never say, "May I ask what this is about?"
- It is general practice in many parts of the world to not call someone who is of considerably higher rank than yourself (thus, a secretary does not normally call a president and ask him or her to return the call).
- Do not routinely use cell phones or other communication devices in the company of others, particularly in more-formal restaurants, theaters, private homes, and when attending business meetings.

We now have a deeper understanding of the key aspects of etiquette, both in the workplace and in our personal lives. But etiquette is also essential for travel, especially business travel. Proper behavior when traveling abroad is the subject of our next chapter.

16

Traveling Abroad

Oscar Wilde once wrote, "The world was my oyster but I used the wrong fork." Business today cannot afford that luxury. We laughed as we watched Julia Roberts in *Pretty Woman*, not knowing what to do at a business dinner. But that was in the movies. In real life, that becomes embarrassing for everyone at the table; it may cost us dearly, even directly resulting in lost business.

When traveling abroad, the very fact of being a foreigner puts us in the limelight. Instead of giving us cause to panic, though, it should be looked upon as a tremendous opportunity. Taking advantage of such opportunity demands that we must know what to do in all circumstances, which includes knowing the social and business customs of the country where you plan to conduct business before you arrive there. Knowing the customs and being aware of the cultural differences not only adds to your confidence, but it can also give you an important edge by allowing you to concentrate on what is said and what is happening, instead of worrying about which fork to use. Of course, paying attention to what is said in social or business circumstances can make a major difference in your ability to negotiate business.

Representing yourself and your company when abroad is as important as a diplomat representing his or her country or large-scale corporate interests.

Be prepared. There is no excuse for bad manners or lack of knowledge about the foreign country in question. The necessary information can be obtained quite easily from bookstores, libraries, embassies, the Department of Commerce, the State Department, the Federal Reserve, and a number of trade and industry organizations. Of course, your company and the Internet may also have useful information.

Knowledge of the foreign country's geography, and not only calendar history but also economic history, is mandatory. We recommend becoming familiar with the country's current economic statistics, which will provide a wealth of data from which important conclusions can be drawn. You must also know about the general political system of the country. To acquire all this advance information does not mean that it must be used at all times. On the contrary, being armed with good background information makes it possible to be considerate, to show respect, and to avoid offending. After all, when we travel in a foreign country, we are guests of that country, and it is worth keeping that in mind at all times.

We are very fortunate that English is a world language. On top of that, our neighboring countries use world languages as well; namely, Spanish, English, and French. (German is the fourth world language.) We must realize the likelihood that no single culture will dominate the foreseeable future in the way that Europe dominated the past several centuries and the United States has dominated the past hundred years or so. Considering the low cost and broad availability of technology—which is the major driving force of all social change, combined with demographic and economic growth—it is reasonable to expect that the twenty-first century (and beyond) will experience China, in particular, and also India, as major players in world affairs. Western civilization will eventually lose market share and no longer dominate. One day, it may be as important to be fluent in Mandarin as in English, which is currently the dominant world language. It is obvious that, as time goes by, it will become more and more important for us Americans to individually master all the world languages, and then some. But speaking a foreign language does not guarantee success. We must be in tune with the way foreigners think and with their mind-sets. Our competitors try. If necessary, we can always use an interpreter, who is a tool, not a partner. In key negotiations, you should bring your own interpreter when you cannot understand the language spoken in the country you are visiting. (The interpreter translates our statements into the home language, and translates the home language into our language, whether English or another.)

Key Points of Etiquette

Here are some general rules to consider when traveling abroad to represent yourself, your corporation, or your political affiliation:

- It is important to maintain a degree of formality and respect.
- To become too familiar too quickly is not always appreciated; do not think all people want to be your new best friend.
- Listen to those around you.
- Be aware of the degrees of sounds and watch what is going on; loud voices are considered obnoxious and are not called for in most situations.
- Listening is an art; listen to what is said, and notice what is not said, by the persons with you.
- Silence can be very powerful, and it is considered respectful in some countries.
- Know that business does not end when you leave the office or the conference room.
- Styles and cultures differ greatly from country to country; as an example, to treat alike the business cultures of India, China, Japan, England, France, Spain, Germany, and Brazil could lead to disaster and lost profits. History, tradition, and language may make the advice in this book readily usable. A case in point is India where the official language is English. Hindi is the second official language but it is sparsely used in South India.

- Conduct yourself with dignity; do not start making jokes or do a lot of teasing.
- Make an effort to eat the food served, and remember that most companies are doing their best to give you the best they and their culture have to offer.
- Never criticize the conditions of a foreign country to its inhabitants; praise where praise is due, as that will go a long way—remember Montesquieu: "we judge people based upon the esteem they show us"—whether we like it or not, the principle of reciprocity is in full force; we like to be praised, and we respond by liking those who praise us.

The Perennial Importance of Proper Communication

It is critical to understand the effectiveness of communication. There is much to be gained, not only with respect to image but also when it comes to relationships, from taking the time to go a step further in communication skills, and that is investing in cultural understanding through cross-cultural training. The dividends can be handsome for any individual, and ultimately, for the company or institution he or she represents, by showing a willingness to become proficient in the development of skills necessary for working or living abroad.

Etiquette Abroad

The etiquette rules described in part 4 are in almost every sense accepted internationally. However, let's comment on some further foreign commonalities and some taboos:

- It is appropriate and polite when addressing a foreign business connection to use such English titles as *Dr./Mr./Mrs./Miss,* plus the last name; or use *Sir* or *Madam.*
- In France, *Monsieur* is both an expression of respect and a title (*Mr.*); for example, *Monsieur le directeur* (managing director).
- *Madame* and *Mademoiselle* stand for *Mrs.* and *Miss,* respectively.
- In Spanish, the equivalent terms are *Señor, Señora,* and *Señorita*; *Don* and *Doña* are used in regard to important or elderly persons, but do not use *Doña* with the first name—only use *Señora* (*Doña Ortiz* but *Señora Elena*).
- German equivalents are *Herr, Frau,* and *Fraulein.* In Japanese *-san* is like our *Mr., Mrs.,* and *Miss,* and it applies to both genders, following the last name, as in *Kobayashi-san.*
- When knighted, an Englishman can use the title *Sir* in front of the name, but never with the last name only. (Therefore, *Sir Elton John* or *Sir Elton,* but not *Sir John.*)
- In France, noblemen are addressed *Monsieur de* _____, in front of the name. While we are

quick to use first names here in the United States, that is not the case abroad.

- In languages other than English, the familiar address is also described through use of informal pronouns for *you* (such as *tu* in French and Spanish, and *du* in German and the Scandinavian languages); we do not recommend using this more informal, and hence more intimate, form of address.

- If the foreigner does not take the initiative, we suggest sticking with the formal terms of address; it is easier to become less formal in countries like England, Spain (among equals), Singapore, and Latin America; in any case, try to remember the names of those you meet—the constant use of *you* when unable to remember a name is not very polite.

- In England, people need to be introduced; as opposed to our custom in the states, where we introduce ourselves.

- When meeting and leaving, a handshake is used in Germany, Italy, Spain, Scandinavia, and Latin America.

- In France, but less so in England, it is common to shake hands at the first encounter; whereas a handshake is less common in countries like Holland and Japan (in Japan, bowing is preferred).

- When with Middle Easterners, use only the right hand to great others, to hand over documents, and to eat.

- It is polite when offering your business card to a Japanese person to hand it with both your hands and to present it with the Japanese print up; do not pull cards from your pocket; use a case.

- When receiving a business card, show respect by reading it; a person's last name is more important than the company name.

- Ordinarily, the Chinese do not use business cards; however, that does not preclude use of business cards by visitors.

- Foreign businesspeople and politicians are well dressed, so it is advisable to use our recommendations (see chapter 13); namely, conservative suits in black (for dinner, in particular), blue, or gray, with a white (or light-blue) shirt, and ties in good taste; no brown shoes after six in the evening.

- Unless a foreigner takes off his jacket and suggests we do the same, we should keep our jackets on.

- In the Middle East, it is not appropriate to wear a jacket of another fabric or pattern than the pants.

- In general, foreign businesswomen dress no less conservatively than women do here in the United States.

- American men often touch each other (i.e., putting a hand on the other's shoulder or slapping him on the back); this custom is unacceptable in countries like China, Japan, South Korea, France, and Holland; the same can be said for questions of a personal nature.

- Punctuality is a must in many countries, particularly in Japan, England, Germany, Switzerland, Holland, and Scandinavia.

- In France, Spain, and Italy, it is acceptable to be fifteen to twenty minutes late.
- In the Middle East, the host, as opposed to the guest, can be quite late.
- In Latin America, too, punctuality is not strictly adhered to.
- Invitations to a person's home are not as common abroad as they are here in the states; in France, for example, it would be very unusual.
- In the United States, it is polite to have eye contact with the people you greet or speak with.
- In Latin America, Japan, and several other Asian countries, it is considered aggressive to make eye contact.
- At business meetings here in America, the most important person is placed at the head of the table.
- In Japan, that person sits at the center of the long side of the table.
- It is still not uncommon that agreements are verbal in Japan; Japanese and other East Asians find it confrontational to say no, so do not expect to be told directly that your proposal, for example, is unacceptable.
- Be prepared to spend days with Middle Easterners before negotiations can be concluded, because a meeting will probably begin with food, drink, and socialization; ceremony is important.
- When with the Japanese, in particular, do not point with a finger, only the whole hand.

- Table manners are of course unique in Japan, as compared to the Western hemisphere; as an example, fingers may be used to eat sushi (also popular in South Korea); otherwise, use chopsticks; ladies may take a bite of a sushi piece, but gentlemen should eat it whole.
- Never cross chopsticks, and do not place them on top of a plate or a bowl; instead, lay them together on the table, with the ends on the edge of the plate or the chopstick rest piece.
- Put a soup lid to the right of the bowl, and, when finished, back on the bowl.
- For rice courses with a lid, place the lid to the left of the bowl when eating; never pour anything like soy sauce over your rice.
- If sitting on the floor eating, the right position is to sit on the knees, as if kneeling.
- The rules for dinner conversation in Japan are very different from ours; the host and the guest of honor engage in conversation, while the rest of the party sits quietly, often not even conversing among themselves.
- Do not be surprised if a Japanese person does not open a gift in front of the person who presented it; this is very common.
- Do not recount money and do not bargain about prices, neither of which is common in China and the Germanic countries.
- Contrary to past protocol, it is now acceptable to examine a restaurant check before paying it in Japan;

in Japan, China, and many European countries, no tipping is required.

- Middle Easterners stand closer to each other than we Americans do, but do not back away from a Middle Easterner if you feel he is getting in your face; that is considered a sign of rejection.

- It is not advisable to be joined by women when on a business trip to Saudi Arabia, for instance.

- The table plan in Scandinavia differs from the international one described previously (see chapter 13); in accordance with the latter, the basic rule is that the hostess is always seated to the left of the most-prominent gentleman, while in Scandinavia, the hostess is seated on the right side of that gentleman.

- In Central and Northern Europe, be prepared to be offered *akvavit* (schnapps) at lunch and informal dinners (it should be served with beer, not wine); the glass is filled to the edge, and it is very impolite not to "bottom up" when toasting. (This is not unlike when mao-tai is served in China.)

- In some countries, such as Spain and Mexico, a course is served to all the ladies before the gentlemen, instead of going around the table.

- When served food in Italy, start eating as the food is on your plate, instead of waiting until everybody has been served.

- In Europe, the bread plate may be used for salad, which is eaten together with the main course; salad may also be eaten from the main plate after the main course (not at the same time).

- The American businessman is often aggressive and wants to get to the point early on; with the exception of Germany, France, Holland, and Scandinavia, such a direct approach is not quite as common abroad.

- Be prepared to meet businesspeople who have a great interest in a wide variety of subjects, which can lead to conversations (not penetrating views or arguments) about politics, literature, art, education, social reforms, and so on, in addition to the specific business matter at hand; in this way, you get to know the people you are talking with, beyond the often confining and sometimes superficial interactions of business association.

Even with the idiosyncrasies of foreign countries and other cultures, the pleasant, considerate, and polite person will get along very well, even if mistakes and oversights take place. If combined with genuine interest, much can be accomplished, and if eliminating, or at least minimizing, mistakes, such an individual can become a real success abroad.

Now that we've completed our examination of good manners and the essential role they play in impeccable style—both here at home and abroad—it's time to summarize our discussion as a whole, which we will do in the conclusion that follows.

Conclusion

We are all supposed to produce results, to maximize wealth, to simplify government, and so on. The traditional pursuit of results has little bearing on style and conduct. If we know and can recognize the errors commonly made in conduct, the source of each, and the different forms each may take, we shall be less likely to deceive ourselves or to be deceived by others. We can and ought to make efforts to reach a style of conduct that motivates and persuades others. We now clearly enter an arena of rules: rules of thinking, rules of etiquette, and rules of ethics. This is what this little book has all been about. Our goal has been to simplify, clarify, and entice. Use the rules intelligently, and style and class will be yours. And then you will no longer pray to be surrounded by run-of-the-mill rivals. On the contrary, you will welcome competent competitors, and your organization will prosper.

So the model for success is straightforward: be pleasant, use good manners, be smart, and be honest. Admirable style and impeccable character will follow. After which, the chances are very good for attaining power, money, and class.

At all costs, we must avoid the inconsistency between integrity (which requires courage) and intelligence (which simply requires brains).

When in doubt, return to the advice offered throughout the chapters of this book.

References

Debrett's Peerage. 2001. *Debrett's Handbook.* London: Debrett's Peerage Ltd.

Friedman, Milton. 1962. *Capitalism and Freedom.* Chicago: University of Chicago Press.

Gad, Emma. 1994. *Tact and Tone.* Copenhagen: Nordic Publishing.

Greider, William. 1989. *Secrets of the Temple.* New York: Touchstone.

Humes, James C. 2013. *Churchill.* New York: Stein and Day Publishers.

Jepson, R. W. 1954. *Clear Thinking.* London: Longman's Green and Co.

Jones, W. T., Frederick Sontag, Morton O. Beckner, and Robert J. Fogelin. 1976. *Approaches to Ethics.* New York: McGraw-Hill.

Josephson's Institute of Ethics. *Commentary and Notes.* Los Angeles: Josephson's Institute of Ethics (notes taken).

Oliver, Anne. 2012. *Finishing Touches.* London: Bantam Books.

Parkinson, Cyril. 1957. *Parkinson's Law: And Other Studies in Administration.* Cutchogue, NY: Buccaneer Books.

Peter, Laurence, and Raymond Hull. 1969. *The Peter Principle.* Cutchogue, NY: Buccaneer Books.

Post, Peggy, Anna Post, and Lizzie Post. 2011. *Emily Post's Etiquette.* Scranton, PA: HarperCollins Publishers.

Rand, Ayn, Nathaniel Branden, Alan Greenspan, and Robert Hessen. 1962. *Capitalism.* New York: New American Library/Signet.

Simmons, George F., Carmen Vazquez, and Philip R. Harris. 1993. *Transcultural Leadership.* Houston: Gulf Publishing.

Thouless, Robert H. 1952. *Straight and Crooked Thinking.* London: English Universities Press Ltd.

Townsend, Robert. 1984. *Further Up the Organization.* New York: Alfred A. Knopf.

The Works of Oscar Wilde. 2003. London: Springs Books.

Zraly, Kevin. 2014. *Windows of the World: Complete Wine Course.* New York: Sterling Publishing.

[AUTHORS' NOTE: *The reference section lists the materials from which we have selected themes and passages relevant to our objectives, particularly* Clear Thinking *(Jepson),* Straight and Crooked Thinking *(Thouless), and* Commentary and Notes *(Josephson's Institute of Ethics).*]

Index

A

accompanying, rules of
    etiquette for
    buses/trains/airplanes, 73
    cars, 72–73
    elevators, 72
    lining up, 75
    public greetings, 72
    rank, 69–71
    restaurants, 73–75
    staircases, 72
    theaters, 75
actionable plan, 30
affluence, recipe for bringing
    about, 4
after-dinner coffee (at dinner
    parties), rules of
    etiquette for, 108–109
argument, dishonest tricks in,
    41–47
ashtrays (at dinner parties),
    rules of etiquette for, 96
assertiveness, 51

attire
    etiquette for business
        attire, 76–82
    etiquette for proper attire,
        75–76

B

balanced cash flows, 25
behavior. *See also* ethics/ethical
    behavior
    management behavior, vii
    proper behavior, 65, 114
belonging, as most important
    feature, 5
bread plate (at dinner parties),
    rules of etiquette for, 97
business as usual, as no longer a
    viable option, 3
business attire, rules of
    etiquette for
    emblems, 81
    gentlemen, 76–77
    gloves, 82

hats, 81

jewelry, 80

ladies, 78

morning coat (city dress), 80

overcoats, 82

purses and briefcases, 81

tailcoat (white tie), 79

tuxedo (dinner jacket, black tie), 78–79

C

capital allocation, 25

capital-market, 8, 9

career

importance of loyalty to organization for advancement in, 57

as key characteristic of business environment, vii, 4–7

pursuit of as potentially sacrificing integrity, 53–54

Churchill, Winston, 29

class

as another word for style, viii

components/elements of, 51, 56

clear thinking, 33–34

cocktail parties, rules of etiquette for, 88–89

coffee (at dinner parties), rules of etiquette for, 109

committees, management by, 17–20

common stock, 9

communication

importance of, 40, 119

importance of clear thinking in, 34

companies, categorization of, 5–6

company man, 5

competence, 16, 19, 21, 22

conversation (at parties), rules of etiquette for, 86

cutlery (at dinner parties), rules of etiquette for, 93–94

D

dancing (at dinner parties), rules of etiquette for, 110

deceptive thinking, safeguards against, 31–43

dependability, 55–56

dinner parties, rules of
etiquette for
after-dinner coffee,
108–109
ashtrays, 96
bread plate, 97
cutlery, 93–94
dancing, 110
entering dining room to
start meal, 90
expressing thanks, 111
filling glasses, 101
finger bowls, 97
finishing dinner and
leaving dining
room, 108
glasses, 95
leaving, 111
menu, 96–97
name cards, 97–98
napkins, 96
plates, 95
recap of some rules about
coffee, 109
serving, 98–99
serving temperature for
wine, beer, and
liquor, 101
speeches, 102
table manners, 104–107

table plan, 90–92
table setting, 92–93
tablecloth, 96
toasts, 103
welcome drinks, 89
wine bottles, 97
wines, 100–101
discreetness, 57
doing the right thing, 52

E

emotional thinking, 33–34, 36
ethics/ethical behavior
integrity, 51–54
loyalty, 57–58
price for being ethical, 53
promise making/promise
keeping, 55–56
role of in decision
making, 53
what not to do, 59–61
etiquette
for accompanying, 69–75
for business attire, 76–82
importance of mastering
rules of, 66
for parties and
entertaining,
83–111

for presenting
(introducing),
68–69
for proper attire, 75–76
tactfulness and good
manners, 65–66
telephoning, 113–114
in traveling abroad, 118–
119, 120–126
visiting cards, 112–113
experience curve, 25

F

fallacies, 26–27
farmer, as category of
companies, 5
finger bowls (at dinner parties),
rules of etiquette for, 97
foreign countries
etiquette when traveling
in, 118–119,
120–126
importance of proper
communication
when traveling
in, 119
traveling in, overview,
115–117

G

general management, 6–7
Getty, Paul, 59
gifts, bringing of to parties,
rules of etiquette for, 85
glasses (at dinner parties), rules
of etiquette for, 95
good heart, 65
greetings, rules of etiquette for
kissing, 67–68
men hugging each
other, 68
salutations and
handshakes, 67

H

handshakes, in greeting, 67
hierarchical exfoliation, 16
hugging, men hugging each
other in greeting, rules
of etiquette for, 68
Hull, Raymond, 16, 20
human suggestibility, 39
hunter, as category of
companies, 5, 6

I

incompetence, 16, 20, 21

industrial policy, 25–26

integrity, 51–54, 128

intelligence, avoiding
    inconsistency between
    integrity and, 128

interpersonal skills, as
    transforming potential
    performers into
    superstars, 7

introducing (presenting), rules
    of etiquette for

    groups, 69

    individuals, 68

invitations (to parties), rules of
    etiquette for, 83–84

K

kissing, rules of etiquette for in
    greeting, 67–68

L

languages, use of in traveling
    abroad, 116–117

leadership

    as binary issue, 14

common flaws in, 14–15

defined, 13

hierarchical exfoliation, 16

as key characteristic
    of business
    environment, vii,
    13–16

key elements of, 16

loyalty, 57–58

M

management behavior, as key
    characteristic of business
    environment, vii

management by committee,
    17–20

management environment

    management by
        committee, 17–20

    stakes and career, 3–9

Managerial Imperative, 20–22,
    27, 53

manners, 61, 65–66, 104–107.
    See also etiquette

menu (at dinner parties), rules
    of etiquette for, 96–97

model for success, 127

money, as impediment, 26

moral principles, 52

N

name cards (at dinner parties), rules of etiquette for, 97–98

napkins (at dinner parties), rules of etiquette for, 96

nonrational sources, deriving opinions from, 36

P

Palle Principle, 22

Parkinson, Cyril, 20, 21

Parkinson's Law, 20

Parkinson's pyramid, 20

parties, rules of etiquette for

arriving for the party, 85

bringing gifts, 85

cocktail parties, 88–89

conversation, 86

dinner parties, 89–111

invitations and RSVPs, 83–84

smoking, 87

personal conduct, importance of, 3

Peter, Laurence, 16, 20, 21

Peter Principle, 20

The Peter Principle (Peter and Hull), 16

plates (at dinner parties), rules of etiquette for, 95

presenting (introducing), rules of etiquette for

groups, 69

individuals, 68

Pretty Woman (film), 115

product programs, 25

product-market, 8–9

promise making/promise keeping, 55–56

proper attire

blazers, 76

general rules, 75

proper behavior, 65, 114

propaganda, 35–36, 40

R

reliability, 55, 56

repeated affirmation, 39, 42

right thing, doing of, 52

risk taking, lack of as willful act, 21

Roberts, Julia, 115

role models, 55

RSVPs (to parties), rules of etiquette for, 83–84

rules

    of etiquette. *See* etiquette

    as not always having to be
        followed literally,
        viii

S

salesmanship

    fundamentals of, 10

    as having a running
        contest with
        adversity, 12

    as not a monologue, 11

    quality and effectiveness
        of application of,
        10–11

    as relying on
        suggestion, 11

salutations, in greeting, 67

serving (at dinner parties), rules
    of etiquette for, 98–99

shepherd, as category of
    companies, 5, 6

smoking (at parties), rules of
    etiquette for, 87

specialist, despecializing
    of, 6–7

specialization, as route to the
    top, 6

staff reviews, 18, 28

stakes, 3–4

strategic planning, 23, 25, 29

strategy

    bad definition of, 29

    business value, 30

    errors in judgment
        as impacting
        formulation of,
        24–25

    as key characteristic
        of business
        environment, vii,
        23–29

    versus tactics, 23–30

style

    as about standing out as
        exceptional, 66

    importance of focusing
        on, 3–4

    as providing key to
        effectiveness, viii

    results of, 7

success, model for, 127

suggestion, 11, 36–40, 42

supercompetence, 16

T

table manners (at dinner parties), rules of etiquette for, 104–107

table plan (at dinner parties), rules of etiquette for, 90–92

table setting (at dinner parties), rules of etiquette for, 92–93

tablecloth (at dinner parties), rules of etiquette for, 96

tabloid thinking, 43

tactfulness, 65–66

tactics
as key characteristic of business environment, vii
strategy versus, 23–30

tax code, as impediment, 26

teamwork, 15

telephoning, rules of etiquette for, 113–114

thanks (at dinner parties), rules of etiquette for, 111

toasts (at dinner parties), rules of etiquette for, 103

traveling abroad
etiquette for, 118–119, 120–126
overview, 115–117

Truman, Harry, 15

V

visiting cards, rules of etiquette for, 112–113

W

Wilde, Oscar, 115

wine bottles (at dinner parties), rules of etiquette for, 97

wines (at dinner parties), rules of etiquette for, 100–101

winning, viii, 7–9, 26